A RHYME, RHYMES AND HALF A RHYME

A COLLECTION OF POEMS
CELEBRATING
THE BOOK OF DANIEL

C. S. Morrison

First published in the United States in 2017 by *CreateSpace Independent Publishing Platform* on behalf of *QualiaFish,* UK

This UK Edition was published in the United Kingdom in 2018 by *QualiaFish* Publications

Copyright © Colin S. Morrison 2017

C. S. Morrison has asserted his moral right to be identified as the author of this work in accordance with the 1988 Copyright Designs and Patents Act (UK).

All rights reserved. No part of this publication may be reproduced, stored in a retrieval system or transmitted in any form or by any means, electronic, mechanical, photocopying, recording or otherwise, without the publisher's prior permission.
This book is sold subject to the condition that it shall not, by way of trade or otherwise, be lent, resold, hired out, or otherwise circulated without the publisher's prior consent in any form of binding or cover other than that in which it is published and without a similar condition including this condition being imposed on the subsequent purchaser.

This book is a work of poetry.
Whilst it is also intended to accurately communicate scholarly observations, neither the author nor the publisher accept liability for any loss arising from reliance on information within it that turns out to be inaccurate.
All quotations in this book are from works that are in the Public Domain.
All Bible text is derived from the World English Bible (WEB) translation, which is in the Public Domain. Observations inserted in square brackets are my own.

ISBN: 978-1-9993393-4-0

ABOUT THE AUTHOR

Colin S. Morrison is a physics graduate, science-writer, philosopher and theologian with a lifelong interest in the book of Daniel. He is the author of *The Blind Mindmaker*, a scientific attempt to explain consciousness, and *Unexpectedly Foretold Occurrences*, which presents in full his observations about the book of Daniel and the current scholarly positions on its prophecies. Puzzled by the incompleteness and odd assumptions inherent in the mainstream account of Daniel 7 and Daniel 9, and concerned that pressure from religious or anti-religious institutions has led scholars to misinterpret these passages, he has spent the last ten years examining the evidence to identify the view that a scientist under no such pressure would regard as most justified.

His conclusions differ radically from those of both critical and conservative scholars. Whilst accepting the mainstream (critical) viewpoint that *Daniel* was completed in the mid-160s BC, he argues that by far the most reasonable interpretation of Daniel 2, Daniel 7 and Daniel 9 is that these passages were included by the book's compiler to *predict the distant future of his own time* (their purpose being to counter skepticism about the book's authenticity). He suspects they were from a source the compiler, with the benefit of hindsight, believed to be a *genuine seer* – even Daniel himself. And he thinks later events have proven that compiler to be correct.

The poems in this book are inspired by the astonishing accuracy of these genuine predictions. They celebrate the spooky fact that this accuracy applies to their most defensible interpretations. It cannot be put down to selective reading. And since the predicted events are both rare and momentous, one can all but rule out chance and self-fulfilment, making it a truly remarkable phenomenon.

> "*Daniel* was in the greatest credit amongst the Jews,
> till the reign of the Roman Emperor Hadrian:
> and to reject his Prophecies, is to reject the Christian religion.
> For this religion is founded upon his Prophecy
> concerning the Messiah"
>
> *Sir Isaac Newton (1643-1727)*

> "None of the prophets has so clearly spoken concerning Christ as has this prophet Daniel. For not only did he assert that He would come, a prediction common to the other prophets as well, but also he set forth the very time at which He would come. Moreover, he went through the various kings in order, stated the actual number of years involved, and announced beforehand the clearest signs of events to come."
>
> *St Jerome (347-420 AD)*

To Fiona, with love

CONTENTS

Introduction: Why Daniel?   1.

PART 1. EMPIRES AND FAITHS   13.

1. **Lamassu**   15.
2. **Dobiel (Bear God)**   18.
3. **The Leopard**   20.
4. **The Monster Unnamed**   22.
5. **The Statue**   27.
6. **Warharan versus Dionysus**   32.

PART 2. ASTONISHING TIMES   37.

7. **The U.F.O.**   39.
8. **A Rhyme, Rhymes and Half a Rhyme**   42.
9. **Hard Times**   46.
10. **A Jubilee Sandwich**   49.
11. **The Anointed One (Christ)**   52.
12. **The End Determined**   57.

PART 3. PEOPLE AND PLACES   63.

13. **The Dying Hadrian's Address to his Soul**   65.
14. **Nehemiah's Defence**   66.
15. **The Clock**   69.
16. **Vespasian**   70.
17. **Josephus' Insistence on Rome**   75.
18. **Darius the Mede**   76.

	PART 4. HYPOTHESES	81.
19.	**The Document**	83.
20.	**Persia (Paarsa)**	86.
21.	**Porphyry's View of the Leopard**	87.
22.	**The Critical Consensus**	88.
23.	**The Historical Preparation**	94.
24.	**The Rock**	99.

APPENDIX: ANNOTATED BIBLE TEXTS	101.
The Statue Dream (Daniel 2:31-45)	103.
The Four Monsters Dream (Daniel 7:1-28)	105.
The Seventy 'Sevens' Prophecy (Daniel 9:24-27)	109.
The Ram and Goat Vision (Daniel 8:1-26)	111.
From Alexander to Antiochus IV (Daniel 11:2-28)	115.
Antiochus IV Epiphanes (Daniel 11:29-12:12)	119.

INTRODUCTION: WHY DANIEL?

The book of Daniel is an astonishing text. It has fascinated me for most of my adult life, and it did the same for such intellectual giants as Sir Isaac Newton, St Jerome, Josephus and Porphyry. My own interest in this text began in my third undergraduate year at St Andrews University. Driven by a string of strange coincidences, I had decided to become a Christian, and was persuaded (by others) that a Christian ought to read the Bible. I was somewhat reluctant at first, being fairly sure that much of the Old Testament wasn't accurate history. It certainly opened with some pretty implausible assertions. As such, I felt it was probably quite irrelevant. For me, Christianity meant the teachings of Jesus (love your neighbour, do good to your enemies, believe that Jesus was from God, etcetera), not the ten commandments, creation myths or the history of the Israelites. But one thing that did intrigue me was prophecy.

There was a lot of it in the Old Testament, and I had heard people say that much of it pertained to Christ. So I did wonder if there were any specific prophecies that could be confidently accepted as having been written prior to the events they predicted. Their prior existence could perhaps be demonstrated via supportive archaeology or allusions to them in datable sources. Such prophecies could constitute *hard objective evidence* supporting Christian claims. My new faith could be *fully justified* – if they exist, that is.

To find out, I went through the Old Testament highlighting all the prophecies that were claimed to be about the writer's distant future. Rather disappointingly, although there were a lot that seemed to be about Christ, none of these supplied specific details that could be used to fix the predicted events to within a relatively narrow window of time. As a science student, I felt that this requirement was essential if any claims to their fulfilment were to be regarded as interesting. After all, given enough time, anything possible can occur. All the prophecies I encountered did not stipulate *when* the predicted events were to take place, and their fulfilment, in my opinion, could not therefore be regarded as anything surprising. That was until I got to the second chapter of the book of Daniel.

There at last I found a prophecy that *did* satisfy my criterion. The event it predicted did lie within a restricted window of time – **that of the kings of the fourth world-dominant empire from the time of Daniel**. And although that window was relatively large, it was an exceedingly rare and unlikely event. The passage predicted the establishment of an 'eternal kingdom' to be given to a 'holy people'. But more importantly, it illustrated this with the image of a rock *cut from a mountain* 'not by hands' being thrown against the symbol of that fourth empire, pulverising it to dust (followed by the symbols of the previous empires), and then growing into *a mountain filling the whole world*. It was immediately apparent to me that if these mountains were to represent anything that was historical, they had to stand for *religions*. After all, political empires pass away. Although religions do too, they certainly have a lot more staying-power. Since this was a Jewish prophecy it was a safe bet that the pre-existent mountain represented *Judaism*.

Hence the passage clearly predicted that **a successful new religion** (the world-filling mountain) would be **formed out of Judaism** at the time of **the kings of the fourth world-dominant empire from the date of the vision** – a religion that should still be around today.

That immediately made me think of Christianity, and this view was further strengthened by my discovery that there was a more detailed version of this prophecy later in the book (Daniel 7) where the king of that 'eternal kingdom' is depicted as a *'son of man'* who gets *enthroned next to God*, and who is to be *'worshipped by all peoples'*. The question was: did Christianity arise within the specified window of time? Did that world-conquering new version of Judaism – an extremely rare phenomenon – arise during the dominance of *the fourth empire from the date of those visions*?

The interpreter of the vision in Daniel 2 said that the first kingdom was 'You O king' (addressing the king of Babylon), which clearly indicated that it was the *Babylonian empire*. And it was evident later in the book of Daniel that Babylon fell to *Persia*. The writer of Daniel 6 and 8 rightly understood the empire that conquered Babylon to be forged by two nationalities – the Medes and the Persians – with the *Persians* being the dominant people at the time of Babylon's fall. Although the person who was 'made king of Babylon' immediately after its fall is a mysterious Mede by the name of Darius, this person appears to have been 'made king' (presumably by somebody else), and in Daniel 6 he rules according to *Medo-Persian laws* – laws that he is *afraid to break*. A quick look at established history shows why. The conquest of the Babylonian empire was really conducted by the *Persian* emperor Cyrus who had taken the Median throne a decade previously. This Darius, if he existed at all, could therefore only have been a puppet ruler under Cyrus' control (which explains his reluctance to break Persian laws, even when tricked into passing them, as in Daniel 6).

So **Babylon** was the *first* of the four world-dominant kingdoms that the prophecy referred to, and **Persia** was definitely the *second*. Moreover, I was well aware that Persia had been famously conquered by the Greek (Macedonian) king Alexander the Great (described as 'the first king of Greece' in Daniel 8). Hence **Greece** (Alexander's empire) had to be the *third* world-dominating kingdom in the sequence. The fourth kingdom must therefore be the empire that conquered Alexander's empire. If that turned out to be **Rome**, the prophecy was indeed an accurate one.

This is where things got a tiny bit more complicated because Alexander's empire actually became split by civil war into *four kingdoms*, two of which (the Ptolemies of Egypt and the Seleucids of Syria) were relatively large empires in their own right. Nevertheless, they were still ruled by *Greek* (Macedonian) kings who saw themselves as Alexander's successors, and who, in the case of three of the empires, descended from generals in *Alexander's army*. For this reason, I was quite satisfied that neither of these Greek empires should be counted as the one to *follow* Alexander's in the sequence. They were clearly still *parts* of that empire, even when they did not get on with each other. And this conclusion appeared to be confirmed by the content of Daniel 7. In that similar prophecy the third empire is **a leopard that has *four wings and four heads***, and the fourth empire a *totally distinct* beast – one that is *'unlike all the former ones'*. It seemed clear to me that the four wings and four heads of that leopard stood for the *four kingdoms* (and *four kingships*) into which Alexander's empire split. Since the fourth empire was to be *totally distinct* (as the text clearly stated), it could only be **the *next* distinct nation to rule the world – the one that would *subdue* those four Greek kingdoms**.

With growing excitement, I realised that this was indeed Rome. If it were possible to show that this prophecy was around in its current form before the beginning of Christianity, I reckoned it had to be considered a genuine fulfilled prediction where the fulfilment was relatively unexpected (and therefore potential evidence of the involvement of a super-human power).

As it turns out, it is! Eight fragmentary copies of this book were found among the Dead Sea Scrolls, and the earliest of these is dated to the late second century *BC* (over a hundred years *before Christ*). Analysis indicates that the book was in its current form at that time. In fact, the content of the book of Daniel itself provides a very good indication of when it reached that current form. Its final prophecy (Daniel 11-12) is a fairly detailed portrayal of the *Syrian wars* between the Seleucid and Ptolemaic parts of Alexander's empire, and it culminates with the campaigns of the Seleucid king Antiochus IV Epiphanes. In particular, it features his persecution of the Jews and defilement of their Temple (which he dedicated to the Greek god Zeus). However, it appears to predict a subsequent campaign of this king that scholars are fairly sure *did not take place*. Since the details in the former part of this prophecy are too accurate to be attributed to chance, scholars rightly date its completion to the time of Antiochus' persecution of the Jews (167-164 BC). And since this prophecy appears to borrow phrases from Daniel 9, and is closely related to Daniel 8, which borrows imagery from Daniel 7, scholars have concluded, very plausibly, that the book was put into its final form at that time. They reckon it was a piece of propaganda designed to boost the morale of the faithful in the face of this dreadful attack upon their religion – a conclusion that is supported by the lack of any allusion to this book in literature written prior to that time. Consequently, we can be very confident that the accurate prophecy in Daniel 2 and Daniel 7 of **a successful new religion formed from Judaism at the time of the kings of the fourth empire in the sequence beginning**

with Babylon *was indeed a prediction from before Jesus Christ!* It cannot possibly have been edited in by hopeful early Christians.

Of course, you might be thinking it was just a bit of a fluke that this prediction came true. Or you might suspect that it probably came true because its fame made people like Jesus try hard to fulfil it (as indeed they did). You might therefore think its fulfilment was not that surprising after all.

I had almost reached that conclusion myself when I discovered that Daniel 7 makes another accurate prediction (*two* more in fact), and in these cases the fulfilment simply cannot be accounted for in either of these ways. Astonishingly, it predicts that **the eleventh king of that fourth empire** would **(1)** *subdue three of the previous ten kings of that empire,* **(2)** *make war on devout followers of the Jewish God and defeat them,* **(3)** *speak boastfully against their God,* and **(4)** *be different from those previous ten rulers.* When you define 'king' in the most logical way as 'a ruler of a nation who has no limit on his time in office', the eleventh king of the Roman Empire was *Vespasian* (the first being *Sulla*). In the light of this, I was totally shocked to discover that Vespasian *succeeded three previous emperors who were all toppled in the same year* (69 AD, known to history as 'the year of the *four emperors*'), and each of these emperors probably did owe his downfall to Vespasian's supporters! Moreover, Vespasian *was* **remembered for religious boasts**. He published several divine omens of himself, and even claimed that a prophecy of the Jewish Messiah spoke of him! He needed to. **Unlike all previous kings of Rome his father was not a senator**. He would therefore have been seen as quite unworthy of the highest office (a little horn indeed). And amazingly, *he did in person* **make war on the Jews and defeat them!** He was also the ruling emperor when the Roman armies destroyed Jerusalem and its Temple in AD 70 – an event many scholars think was pivotal in the rise of Christianity. Intriguingly, that event seems to be explicitly predicted in Daniel 9, which turns out to be an even more fascinating example of accurate prophecy than Daniel 7 is.

Unlike Daniel 7, Daniel 9 does not use a sequence of empires to set the time of its predicted events. Instead, it actually gives *a time interval with a definite starting point* ('the issuing of the word to restore and rebuild Jerusalem', which was in ruins in Daniel's day). Since that starting point is known to within a month or so, the window of time for the fulfilment of the first prediction in Daniel 9 – the arrival of a 'Christ' ('Anointed One') at Jerusalem – is equally specific. Astonishingly, **the most defensible meaning of that time interval predicts an arrival of that Christ as 'exalted prince' in March-April or April-May of 33 AD**, and the former contains the most likely date for the Triumphal Entry of Jesus!

The rest of that prophecy predicts that this Christ would *get killed empty-handed*, that Jerusalem *and the Temple* would later be destroyed, and that after further unrest **a ruler of *the same people who destroyed the temple* would come to Jerusalem and make a public promise that he would keep for the last seven years of his life**. In the middle of those seven years, he would even cause Jewish sacrifice to cease, and raise an idol (an 'abomination of desolation') on an infamous overspreading. **All this was fulfilled by the emperor Hadrian**, who even died exactly seven years after beginning to confirm his public promise to rebuild Jerusalem!

Mainstream scholars currently claim that this prophecy, and also the 'four empires' one found in Daniel 7, were both actually meant to predict the Greek (Seleucid) king of Syria, Antiochus IV Epiphanes. In their view, the writer of those prophecies just made a few rather unlikely mistakes. He mistakenly added an extra empire to Daniel 7, and thoughtlessly split his third – rather than his fourth – into four parts. They even think he accidentally made the time-period in Daniel 9 a couple of centuries too long! However, there is no evidence to support these assertions. In fact, the content of the rest of the book of Daniel soundly refutes them. For example, in Daniel 8 – a vision that clearly depicts Antiochus IV – there is a sequence of just *two* empires, which are helpfully identified as **'Medo-Persia'** and **'Greece'**. The second of these *splits into four parts, just like the third empire in Daniel 7* (with Antiochus IV emerging from one of these parts). Since Babylon isn't depicted in this vision, this sequence of empires is perfectly consistent with the view that **Greece is the *third* empire in Daniel 7**, and ***Rome* the fourth**. And in Daniel 9 the compiler of the book of Daniel appears to have inserted a prayer derived from *the first prayer in the book of Nehemiah*. Since it was in answer to that prayer that Nehemiah was given his *permission to rebuild Jerusalem*, it is very hard to believe that this compiler did not think 'the word to restore and rebuild Jerusalem' (which is the starting point of the time-period in the prophecy of that chapter) was not that very permission. Yet critical scholars never argue for this starting point. In the light of the similarity between those prayers, I think this can only be because the presence of Nehemiah's building work would have constantly reminded the citizens of Jerusalem of the time that had gone by, making it very unlikely that a contemporary of Antiochus IV would get that time wrong by two whole centuries.

What those scholars seem to me to be neglecting is the very real possibility that Daniel 7, Daniel 2, and Daniel 9 were actually *intended as predictions* (just as they appear to be). Their purpose, to my mind, was to stop skeptics arguing that all the prophecies in this book had already been fulfilled (the same purpose critical scholars currently assign to the unknown campaign of Antiochus IV mentioned earlier). Perhaps the compiler even chose those prophecies from an ancient source precisely because they appeared to have started to come true! Their content is actually far more supportive of this hypothesis than of the view that they were just two extremely flawed attempts at predicting Antiochus IV (which would be completely unnecessary in a book that already contains two extremely *good* prophecies of that hated king).

Whatever their origin, though, **the astonishing thing is that they do appear to have come true long after their date of writing. And they are *far too specific and time-limited for us to attribute this accuracy to chance*.** Moreover, the events they predict are not of the sort that human beings could bring about by their own deliberate efforts. The poems in this book are intended to raise awareness of these astonishing and little-appreciated facts.

The poems in *Part 1* were inspired by the wonderful imagery in the visions of Daniel 7, 2 and 8; those in *Part 2* by the mysterious time phrases found in Daniel 12, 7 and 9; the poems in *Part 3* by some of the characters involved or invoked in the interpretation of Daniel's prophecies; and those in *Part 4* by the various explanations for their content and accuracy that scholars have put forward. The gospel quotation in my eighth poem is Matthew 24:15-22, where Christ is shown to endorse Daniel 9 and support the view that it predicted the future in his own day. And the prophecy of Christ in my 23rd poem comes from Isaiah 53.

Although all these poems were composed by me and express my own personal views, my thirteenth poem is my slightly-expanded version of a poem attributed to the emperor Hadrian, the king who fulfilled Daniel 9, by the *Historia Augusta* (a late-Roman history book). I have included it because, for me, it expresses, in a beautiful and mournful way, the far-from-irrational fear of an impoverished afterlife that I believe Christ's offer of eternal life (of the rich, intelligent sort we currently enjoy) is intended to remove. The accuracy of Daniel 2, 7 and 9, and their endorsement of

Christianity, gives me terrific hope that there really is a God who is offering us the chance to ensure that our consciousness (soul) is put back in charge of an intelligent and rational organism at some time in the future – an offer that I have gratefully accepted.

For readers unfamiliar with ancient history, I should briefly point out that my second poem alludes to the victory of Cyrus of Persia over three great emperors: his Median overlord and grandfather Astyages, the Lydian king Croesus, who had taken the field because an oracle had said that if he did so he would destroy a great empire (meaning his own!), and the Babylonian coregent Nabonidus whose son was king Belshazzar of Daniel 5. All three are reported by various sources to have had their lives spared, and been well-treated after their fall. According to Herodotus, Astyages dreamt of his overthrow long before in the form of a vine growing from his daughter's genitalia to fill his empire, and had ordered the boy Cyrus killed. When he discovered that this had not been done, he butchered the son of the general responsible, and had him dine on his son's flesh – causing that general to rebel and back Cyrus.

I should also point out that Josephus, in my 17th poem, is the first-century Jewish historian to whom we owe, not only a very early Jewish interpretation of Daniel, but also a first-hand account of the emperor Vespasian and his rise to power. Porphyry, to whom my 21st poem is dedicated, is the third-century Greek philosopher who first questioned early Christian interpretations of Daniel. And Laenas (in my 17th poem) is the Roman envoy Gaius Popillius Laenas who famously ordered Antiochus IV to abandon his second conquest of Egypt in 168 BC. This latter event is alluded to in Daniel 11:30 because it led to that king's persecution of the Jews. But for me its importance is that it clearly shows the public dominance of Rome at the time Daniel was completed (a dominance that I think is seriously underplayed in the literature).

I have included an annotated translation of the prophecies themselves in the *Appendix* for anyone who wants to easily check these references out, or experience the source of my inspiration at first hand. I strongly recommend it. The translation used is the *World English Bible* (*WEB*) version, though I have inserted my own notes in small square-bracketed text wherever I felt the reader may need further explanation, or where other translations differ significantly from the *WEB* rendering.

My hope is that these poems will inspire you to want to read a more in-depth discussion of these issues, which I have prepared in my recent book *Unexpectedly Foretold Occurrences: Scientific Evidence that there is a God who Loves You (and why scholars don't discuss it)*. The scientific evidence referred to is the accuracy of Daniel 2, 7 and 9 (which goes much deeper than I've described here) and the considerable body of data that supports the view that these prophecies were written in their current form long before the events they predict took place in the specified windows of time.

Although much has been written on the book of Daniel, you will currently be hard-pressed to find any other works that explore the possibility that *these three prophecies were included to provide genuine predictions of the distant future for the purpose of countering skepticism about the late appearance of this book*. Due probably to academic biases, this hypothesis simply doesn't get touched in either mainstream or conservative scholarship. Yet, as I have already explained, there are very good reasons to think it is the correct view. I suspect critical scholars are being put off by the theological implications of the mind-blowing accuracy of these predictions. That stunning precision isn't explainable as hindsight or human effort, and this very reasonable proposal would expose it for all to see. To my mind, that accuracy is an absolutely amazing phenomenon, and the poems in this book openly celebrate it.

The Epicureans are in error, who cast Providence out of human life,
and do not believe that God takes care of the affairs of the world,
nor that the universe is governed and continued in being
by that blessed and immortal nature,
but say that the world is carried along of its own accord,
without a ruler and a curator…
were it destitute of a guide to conduct it, as they imagine,
it would be like ships without pilots,
which we see drowned by the winds,
or like chariots without drivers,
which are overturned;
so would the world be dashed to pieces
by its being carried without a Providence,
and so perish, and come to nought.
So, by the forementioned predictions of Daniel,
those men seem to me very much to err from the truth,
who determine that God exercises no providence over human affairs;
for if that were the case, that the world went on by mechanical necessity,
we should not see that all things would come to pass
according to his prophecy.

Flavius Josephus

(Antiquities of the Jews, Book X, 11:7)

PART ONE

EMPIRES AND FAITHS

1. Lamassu

Rushing toward the dreamer...
Majestic powerful wings...
Eagle feathers shimmer...
A golden mane swings.
Swooshing down, graceful arcs
explode upon the shore.
The beast alights, sheaths its claws,
and emits a mighty roar.

Yet suddenly, out of nowhere —
invisible to the eye —
A pressure grips those giant wings
and rips them to the sky.
The fully feline body
prances round in fear.
But the pressure grips its forelegs
and raises them in the air.

When it's standing on its hindfeet
looking ridiculously tall,
The pressure bursts its chest apart,
sucks out a huge beating heart,
And pops in something small.
From then, its roar becomes a call.

It staggers forth on just two legs,
somewhat like a man.
And a royal proclamation
makes this plain to understand.

Daniel 4 claims to be
the words of a king,
The builder of Babylon,
Famous for its bling.
It tells us he dreamed about
a massive luscious tree
That sheltered all the peoples
in a land of harmony.

A heavenly voice orders
that this tree be chopped right down.
But a stump is to be kept alive,
embedded in the ground.
For seven years
that stump's to have the heart of a beast,
And only when it praises God
is it to be released.

The meaning of this dream
is that this king would become ill —
Drinking dew alone
among wild animals until
He acknowledged God for everything
he'd thought of as his own.
When he did so, he was healed in mind,
and given back his throne.

What happened to the lion
in Daniel 7's dream
Reminds us of this humbling,
with a slightly different theme:
The beast is given a *human* heart,
instead of the reverse.
But here it stands for Babylon,
not the king who had that curse.

Guarding his great palace
with majestic wings of stone,
Carved out of a gigantic rock
by sculptors now unknown,
Were massive lions with human heads –
the gods he thought he knew –
The protective spirit of Babylon:
The divine Lamassu.

Author's Note: All serious scholars accept that the Lion with Eagle's Wings in Daniel 7 represents the Empire of Babylon. It is also widely acknowledged that winged lions regularly featured in the art of that empire. However, scholars appear to me to underplay the significance of the fact that the winged lion (with human head) typically represented a Babylonian *god* – the *Lamassu* (also depicted as a winged bull). That god appears to have been regarded as the spirit who protected the Babylonian kings, and so the winged lion in this dream is very likely to symbolise that protective spirit of the Babylonian Empire. The problem critical scholars have with acknowledging this is that it automatically suggests the beasts representing the subsequent empires *also* signify 'protective deities'. As you will see in Poems 2, 3, 4 and 20, this strongly supports the simple historical view that the sequence is Babylon-Persia-Greece-Rome, and that the vision, whenever it was written, was intended to be a *real prediction*.

2. Dobiel (Bear God)

The leopard rose up from the deep.
The bear before was half asleep –
Three ribs gripped in powerful jaws,
The East controlled by its raised paws.
For two whole centuries it had ruled.
Three emperors it had unstooled,
But kept alive and made to serve
This bear who'd risen with such a nerve:

A grandfather who'd once allied,
And kept awake the sleepy side;
A wealthy king who'd sought advice,
And thought the words he'd heard were nice;
And the lion lord who ruled the South,
Whose son was slain by the ursine mouth,
Who'd allowed his kingdom to decline
And swiftly fall to a menstrual vine.

What the grandfather dreamt came true.
His downfall was a gruesome stew,
And a grandson whom he'd thought was dead
Was invited to become the head.
Those three kings whom he kept alive
Witnessed his meteoric rise.
As grandson to the king before
He ruled both sides of the bear.

Yet, like most who rule with war,
Overconfident, he went too far.
And though his successors conquered more,
They were beaten on a western shore.
Forced back not just once but twice,
The East alone must thus suffice.
The bear never ruled the West,
From whence emerged the spotted beast.

Author's Note: It is to my mind extremely difficult to believe the mainstream claim that the bear in Daniel 7, who is *'raised up on one side'* with *'three ribs in its mouth between its teeth'*, was not meant to stand for the two-sided Medo-Persian Empire under the rule of Cyrus the Great of Persia (a king known for sparing the lives of three of the emperors he defeated). Even the choice of animal supports this view. The Jewish writers of the Talmud in the early first millennium accounted for major political events as the result of heavenly warfare between angels who guarded nations. The name *'Dobiel'* (or *Dubbiel*) is the name they gave to the angel who guarded Persia in their theology. It means *'bear god'*. Although the context in which the Talmud refers to this angel clearly supports the view that this choice was influenced by the book of Daniel (rather than the other way round), this choice of name indicates two important things. Firstly, it shows that the Jewish religious leaders of that time clearly interpreted the sequence of empires in Daniel 7 in the way conservative scholars do today: Lion=Babylon, Bear=Persia, Leopard=Greece, Unidentifiable monster=Rome. And secondly, it shows that they regarded the animal symbolism as standing for *protective national deities* (as implied by my suggestion that the winged lion=Lamassu in Poem 1). Although the former observation is not too serious for critical scholars, who can merely argue that this represents a re-interpretation of the prophecy to suit the times in which the Talmud was written, the latter observation, in my opinion, strikes a killer blow. It shows that Jews really did interpret the animals in this dream as *guardian deities* – a very defensible interpretation that we have no reason to think would change as the centuries passed. As you will see in Poem 3, it perfectly explains why a four-headed *leopard* was chosen as the symbol for the *third* empire in the sequence. But it can only do so if that third empire is *Greece* (Alexander's *Macedonian* Empire).

3. The Leopard

Like lightning striking from the West,
Four birdlike wings and spotted chest,
And then, that's strange, four heads appear,
Given power to rule for many a year.

In Pella, where a king was born,
Who'd take the whole known world by storm,
There's found a large mosaic of stone,
Dating from that troubled time.

Side-saddle on a leopard's back
A naked man with a pine-cone stick.
The god of Nysa is his name,
The conquest of India his claim.

That was, at least, until that king
About whom all the bards did sing —
A king who never lost a fight
And set Persepolis alight.

After vanquishing Darius' men,
He invaded India and won,
Returning when his men were done
To suddenly die in Babylon.

He left behind an unborn heir
Who never would receive a share.
His empire into four was split,
So his lords could govern it.

As he reached his teenage years,
He met his end in blood and tears.
His lords fought to avenge his fate,
And unite the empire of The Great.

But all in vain they struggled on.
The empire into four was torn.
The victors made themselves its kings —
A head to each of its four wings.

Yet each of these four heads was crowned
With a diadem based on the mitra band
On the head of the leopard god of wine
Who went to war in leopard skin.

"The Good Deity!" echoed the toast
All along that empire's coast.
When India fell to its commander
"Dionysus!" became "*Alexander!*"

Author's Note: I think the mainstream insistence that the four-headed, four-winged leopard in Daniel 7 was meant to represent Persia rather than *Greece* (the Greco-Macedonian Empire of Alexander the Great) is both incredibly surprising and highly suspicious. The latter had, after all, been divided into *four parts* ruled by *four separate Macedonian dynasties* for many decades prior to the time mainstream scholars believe the book of Daniel was put together, and it is clearly portrayed as such in Daniel 8 and Daniel 11. As the Greek god Dionysus was closely associated with that empire, even the leopardlikeness of that beast can be explained under this view. The problem for mainstream scholars is purely that accepting this would mean that this vision includes a *genuine prediction*; and as Poem 4 reveals, that prediction *really did come true!*

4. The Monster Unnamed

The fourth empire has a different feel.
It follows one that split in four.
It crushes its prey with teeth of steel.
Its bronze claws stamp them to the floor.

Why do mainstream scholars not
Assume that's Rome, as was long thought?
She ruled the world when the book was written.
Its writer knew the Greeks were beaten.

Its unidentifiability
Plausible deniability —
An astute political calculation
To not offend a friendly nation.

But the only empire split in four
Was Alexander's — then no more
Than puppet states at Rome's command
(A fact that scholars must understand).

Of course, that makes it a prediction —
Not hindsight nor historical fiction.
For Rome was a republic then,
And the beast has horns that number ten.

A sequence of kings will come from it;
The eleventh of which will three uproot.
He'll make war on Jerusalem,
And speak against its God to boot.

His little horn grows great in size,
And gains a boasting mouth and eyes.
Sometime later, this beast is slain.
It's kingdom is God's people's gain.

But predictive work should be expected
To stop this book from being rejected.
Skeptics would soon smell a rat
If all its prophecies were not that!

Mainstream scholars must merely fear
This view would damage their career;
Wrongly labelling them, their frightened,
"Conservative" or "unenlightened".

But why? Because that dream came true.
The emperor who first fought the Jew
Three before him overthrew
Within a single year — Not two!

And if, like me, you see a king
As a nation's head with unlimited reign,
He was the eleventh to take the helm
When the western world was a Roman realm.

And he was indeed a boastful man:
Great omens were within his plan
To legitimise his right to rule —
And Jewish scripture a handy tool.

Although many more such kings would pass
Ere a Jewish sect would kick Rome's ass,
Remember that this horn grew thicker,
Which suggests this time would not be quicker.

In fact, it even grew two eyes —
Another king the Jews despise?
Hadrian, by whom they were expelled,
Was famed for touring the lands he ruled.

Although this beast gets killed and burnt,
This can't mean Roman power was spent,
For the beasts of conquered states live on,
Suggesting faiths that hadn't gone.

And if those beasts are faiths, of course,
This dream predicts a revolution.
A faith of clearly Jewish source
Replaces all Rome's contribution.

But why should scholars be worried by that?
Coincidences happen a lot.
The problem is this faith is not
Traditional ancient Jewish thought.

The dreamer sees a 'son of man'
Approach the highest throne of God.
He too is set upon a throne
And worshipped — which is incredibly odd!

The Jews believed in a single God —
The maker of the world for them.
To worship anything else as well
Was sacrilege in Israel.

Hence, the gain these words foretell
Would not have made them quick to sell.
They're not like other Hebrew writing —
Their fulfilment is thus so exciting!

Naturally, the Christian mind
Claims this as something God designed;
And mainstream scholars will not choose
To appear as though they share such views.

But you decide, for that's your right!
You have the data in your sight.
Wouldn't a leopard split four ways
Be the one empire with a four-part phase?

Especially as that empire's shown
As a goat on which four horns have grown
Elsewhere in that very book —
In Daniel 8 — It's worth a look!

And an empire billed as 'more unique
Than all before' — which are 'more weak' —
Would never be seen as one of the bits
Of the empire after which it sits.

And remember, Rome already held sway
When the book was written, so there is no way
The empire stronger than all the rest
Could be anything other than Italy's best.

Hence, there really is no doubt
This dream definitely came about.
The eleventh king ruling the world from Rome
Uprooted three who ruled the same,

And made war on the Jews as claimed,
And blasphemed their God's holy name,
And conquered them, while a mere knight –
A little horn in the Senate's sight.

And believers in the Jewish God,
Who also worshipped another Lord,
Did indeed supplant the faith
Of ancient Romulus's race.

That's astonishing, for this dream was written
Two centuries *or more* before that king –
The eleventh dictator of the Roman nation
To rule the world with unlimited reign.

Author's Note: The match between the eleventh king prediction in Daniel 7 and the events of 69 AD is scarily precise. Three unlimited dictators of the Roman Empire met their ends as the eleventh – a conqueror of Judea – rose to power.

5. The Statue

You looked, O king,
And there before you,
dazzlingly bright,
Stood a huge metal statue,
glinting in the light:
A head of gold, chest of silver,
arms of silver too,
Bronze thighs and belly, iron legs,
and feet with clay mixed through.

You watched, O king,
And from a mountain,
cut out without hands,
A rock gets hurled against the statue.
On its feet it lands.
Gold, silver, bronze, iron and clay
disintegrate and blow away.
But the rock becomes a mountain that
o'er all the world extends.

You are, O king,
That head of gold,
dazzling to the eye.
God gave you power, strength and glory.
It's you all men obey.
After you will come a kingdom,
inferior to yours;
And then a third, the rule of which
the whole earth endures.

You saw, O king,
The iron legs,
and feet of iron and clay:
A fourth kingdom, strong as iron,
will break all in its way;
So it will crush and break the others,
but will in time grow weak.
Its intermarried peoples
will not together keep.

Know, O king,
That at the time
those latter monarchs rule,
God will set up a kingdom
that will never ever fall!
It will break those other kingdoms,
and end them all for sure;
But will itself, forever and ever,
prosper and endure.

That's why, O king,
You saw that rock
cut out without hand,
Hurled against the statue,
on its feet to land —
The rock that pulverised the metal
against which it was hurled,
And became a massive mountain
that filled the entire world.

Think, O reader!
That king ruled Babylon —
the head
(Which had to seem superior,
or Daniel would be dead!).
Since Persia conquered Babylon,
she's the arms and chest.
But the kingdom that came next
seems to have done the best.

That's why, O reader,
That third kingdom
has to be Greece.
Persia famously failed to rule
the people of the West.
Hence, the only empire ancients held
to rule the whole earth
Was that of Alexander,
prior to his death.

Which means, O reader,
The fourth empire
has to be Rome!
The iron legs the Republic.
The feet a time to come,
When the Roman Empire would be ruled
by a line of powerful kings,
Her peoples being a mixture
whose loyalty often swings.

Of course, O reader,
That time
has now long come to pass.
And it probably wasn't something
that couldn't have been guessed.
But the rock that broke the statue
into chaff the wind did scatter —
The rock that birthed a mountain —
is a very different matter.

Know, O reader,
This mountain
can only be a faith —
An eternal worldwide kingdom,
established by a God.
And the mountain that it came from —
Make no mistake —
Can only be Judaism
(even if Dan. 2 were fake).

Hence, O reader,
This passage says,
when Rome, by kings, is ruled,
A faith formed from Judaism
will conquer the whole world —
A faith founded by its God,
just as Jesus Christ
Founded Christianity
from the Judaism of the East.

Take note, O reader,
This passage
cannot have been written
Later than the time
Rome's Republic held sway.
Its prediction of this Jewish sect
by which the world is smitten
Is an astonishing flash of foresight
one would *not* expect to see!

Author's Note: The significance of the two mountains in the vision of Daniel 2 is rarely noted by mainstream scholars. This dream does not predict the conquest of the world by traditional Moses-based Judaism – the religion being suppressed by the Greek king of Syria at the time the book of Daniel was put together (around 165 BC). If that had been the intention *no second mountain would have grown out of the divinely cut rock*. The first mountain (obviously representing the Mosaic religion), not the rock cut from it, would itself have grown to fill the world. The fact that there *is* a second mountain growing out of the rock makes it unquestionable that this dream was meant to predict the emergence of a new and distinct religion from Moses-based Judaism – and one that was in God's eyes truer. This is made even clearer by the image of the 'son of man' being enthroned next to God and 'worshipped by all peoples' in the alternative version of this prophecy found in Daniel 7. Although the suppression of Judaism at that time no doubt gave rise to new ideas, one would hardly think such a "heretical" suggestion would be supported by the Jewish resistance – unless, of course, it was already enshrined in scripture. Alternatively, it may have been allowed because it was a prediction about the *distant future* (not the "righteous" Judaism of 165 BC). The fact that this event is set to happen during the reign of *kings of the fourth world-dominant empire from Daniel's time* definitely puts it way beyond 165 BC. Even ignoring the all-but-conclusive evidence in Daniel 7, it is obvious that the third empire in this vision is Greece. Greece had famously escaped Persian rule, so in the second century BC Persia would never have been described as 'ruling the whole earth'. And although Rome had already crushed all the Greek kingdoms, she was at that time a fierce and proud republic. Any kings were yet to come (and would not have seemed likely any time soon).

6. Warharan versus Dionysus

Before the river stood the ram.
The two horns on its head were high.
But one was higher — not the same.
The bear was probably to blame!

The writer of Daniel 8
Saw the bear in Daniel 7.
And sought to re-create —
To make his dream seem more from heaven.

The bear was raised up on one side —
Three ribs clamped between its teeth.
He thought another bear not wise,
And the ribs weren't relevant at its death.

Yet 'one side higher than the other'
Suggesting Persia's domination
Over the Medes, who once were stronger,
Was a good symbol of that nation.

But a raised side of a different beast?
A far too obvious derivation.
Skeptics would, at the very least,
Decry God's lack of innovation.

So instead, that night he went to bed
And woke up with a bright idea.
He'd have two horns on some beast's head
And a difference in their heights appear.

But then, what animal should he use?
He knew the bear stood for a god —
The angel Dobiel to the Jews.
But a bear again would cry of fraud.

So he thought of Zarathustra —
The hymns he'd heard the Persians sing;
The most popular being to Verethragna,
The best-armed god who wasn't the King.

That god, he'd heard, had ten known forms,
Four of which were wild beasts,
And one a ram with two long horns —
That one he felt by far the best.

With wild beauty and free of care,
A ram was also domesticated.
But didn't serve to pull or bear —
A force both free and sophisticated.

He'd already thought of the contender:
A he-goat with a *single* horn —
What better symbol of Alexander?
Dionysian goat-cum-unicorn.

Like the leopard in Daniel 7,
Yes, the goat stood for that god.
He also flew — Alexander's swiftness —
Though four wings were felt too odd.

Yet four-part symbolism is included:
The horn for Alexander breaks,
And four horns from its stump protruded,
Each of which a kingdom makes.

From one of these there comes a branch
That's small but grows in power.
To south and east and up to heaven,
The writer has it tower.

It casts down some of the stars to earth
And tramples them underfoot,
Opposes God, for what it's worth,
And the Temple's given to it.

It's clear this is Antiochus the Fourth —
No interpretation's needed —
Daniel 11's 'king of the north'
By whom the Jews were badly treated.

But it's not clear why this dream was made.
For *Eleven* says the same —
In more detail there, this theme's portrayed.
Could *Seven* be to blame?

For it has *four* enormous beasts,
And here there's only *two*;
And the matching symbolism insists
The fourth beast ain't in view.

This ensures the reader sees that beast
Foretelling a *future* thing,
And won't reject this book till at least
Rome's fall or twelfth king.

Though skeptics may proclaim all day
That *Daniel* still seems fake.
Others will point to Daniel 7
And say, "Give us a break!

This prophecy is *not* about
Our sufferings right now.
A forger would have left it out
In case it didn't come true!"

Surprisingly, this obvious theory
Has never been suggested.
Perhaps because no scholar wants
That oracle to be tested!

For unlike the horns in Daniel 8,
The horns on that fourth beast
Are eleven kings, the eleventh of which
Makes three before deceased;

And makes war on the Jewish state;
And speaks against their God;
And defeats them (like the one they'll hate);
And tries to change their laws.

Yet sometime after that emperor
A faith formed by a Jew
Replaces the one this beast stands for.
And all these things came true!

Author's Note: Like Daniel 11, the vision in Daniel 8 identifies the empires of Greece and Persia *by name*, and it also ends with a detailed portrayal of the Greek king of Syria, Antiochus Epiphanes, his plundering of the Jerusalem Temple, and his attempts to abolish the Jewish religion. Even those of us who believe in divinely-inspired prophecy should be suspicious of this one. Although the Jewish God *might* want to warn his people of such impending troubles, would that God make it so easy to work out when those events would transpire (thereby endangering the prophecy's fulfilment) by naming the nations to come? Wouldn't such a prophecy have caught the attention of the Persian authorities during the two centuries in which they ruled over Judea, prompting them to mount an even greater effort to wipe Greece off the map? And would it not have become incredibly famous towards the end of the fourth century BC for its astonishingly accurate portrayal of Alexander's conquest of Persia, his untimely death, and the four-way splitting of his empire? There is no hint of such fame, or even of the prophecy's existence, prior to the 160s BC. Moreover, although it is supposedly set a mere two years after the vision of Daniel 7, and under the same Babylonian regime, it is written in a *different language*. Daniel 7 is in Aramaic, whereas Daniel 8 is in Hebrew (just like Daniel 11). Since the focus of Daniel 8 – King Antiochus Epiphanes' persecution of the Jews – is the same as that of Daniel 11, we should suspect it probably came from the same author. Judging from the detailed history evident in Daniel 11, and the fact that Daniel 11 appears to incorporate failed guesswork about a final campaign of Antiochus Epiphanes, that author was almost certainly an educated Jewish contemporary of that king writing sometime between 167 and 164 BC – probably to boost the morale of the beleaguered Jewish faithful. However, for his ruse to succeed, his audience had to believe his book was authentic. It couldn't just predict events that had already happened, or were likely to happen soon. This is probably why he included the genuine prophecies found in Daniel 2, 7 and 9. His creation of Daniel 8 seems to me to be designed to make it explicitly clear to his readers that Daniel 2 and 7 predict events *well beyond their day*. But it also makes it clear to *us* that these prophecies are genuine. It shows us that they existed in 165 BC, and that their perfect fulfilment is therefore *totally inexplicable*.

PART TWO

ASTONISHING TIMES

7. The U.F.O.

Hovering bright above the river —
Metallic limbs and torch-like eyes.
Down my spine there crept a shiver:
A messenger from the skies!

In starlight suits his two companions
Guarded each bank of the stream.
The nearest called to the fiery-eyed one:
"How long to fulfil the dream?"

I raised my head in expectation.
A burning glare pierced my eye.
And in a voice of revelation,
There thundered a reply:

"I swear by Him who lives forever —
He who is above the sky,"
The voice drowned out the rushing river,
"I bring you truth, I do not lie!

For a time, two times and a half
Is how long those wonders take.
All these things will be completed
When God's people's strength does break."

'For a time, two times and a half?'
Is that a riddle I must solve?
Is this alien having a laugh?
I gathered my resolve.

"I do not understand", I ventured.
Fires blazed. I braced to die.
The thunder boomed like a dam that's ruptured:
"The words are sealed till the end is nigh!

From the time the sacrifice is taken,
And the abomination raised,
There shall be — Be not mistaken —
One thousand, two hundred and ninety days!

Blessed is he who's still alive —
He who reaches the happy day —
One thousand, three hundred and thirty-five,
After sacrifice is taken away."

"Of course!", I thought, for then it struck me:
"The 'times' are 'years'. I should have known!"
Nebuchadnezzar, he was lucky!
For just seven *years* his mind was gone.

But then, that was ancient history —
Four hundred years ago or more.
This vision, till now, had been no mystery.
But would the Temple be restored?

That is what we all were sensing.
The king who hated us would fall,
And God's Temple get a cleansing
When I, "Daniel", would call.

But what if this were *just* a dream?
Or what if I've been duped by lies?
Those three may not be who they seem.
Should I really trust my eyes?

I collapsed with sudden doubt and weakness.
Am I truly such a fool?
But as I drifted into darkness,
I knew I had the perfect tool.

Author's Note: Wherever the inspiration for the lengthy vision and prophecy of Daniel 10-12 came from, we can be quite certain that the person who received it was not living in the sixth century BC. It presents so many obvious details of the first six *Syrian wars* – the conflicts between the Seleucid and Ptolemaic parts of Alexander's empire – that had it been written prior to the second century BC it would undoubtedly have become extremely famous. The Seleucid and Ptolemaic kings would have spared no expense to acquire copies, which would inevitably have fallen into the hands of Greek historians. The fact that there is no hint of it in works written prior to the 160s BC therefore strongly supports the highly defensible mainstream view that it was written between 167 and 164 BC as propaganda to boost the morale of the Jewish faithful. The Jews in Jerusalem were at that time undergoing severe persecution at the hands of the Seleucid king Antiochus Epiphanes who aimed to stamp out their religion. If they kept their laws, they risked death. Daniel 10-12 seems to have been written in a bid to persuade them that this risk was worthwhile. It promises a resurrection and everlasting life and honour for those who hold firm to the end. It is pseudonymously presented as the last great writing of a prophet who lived four hundred years before to give those promises the authority of a God who knows the future. Does that mean God wouldn't want it in the Bible? I say no. It has been kept in the book of Daniel precisely because its date of authorship is obvious. God wants us to see that it is a forgery and use it to show the doubters that the prophecies of Christ and Christianity in Daniel 2, 7 and 9 were definitely predictions at the time the book of Daniel was put together. As poems 8, 9 and 10 imply, its opportunistic interpretation of the time period in Daniel 7 may even have made that prophecy less of a liability under the later *Roman* persecutions.

8. A Rhyme, Rhymes and Half a Rhyme

When the abomination of desolation
Of which the prophet Daniel spoke
Stands upon the holy mountain
(Understand — this is no joke!)
If you're in Judea, flee!
To the mountains far away!
If you're on your housetop, stop!
Leave what's in your home or shop!
If you're in your field at work
Don't go back for cloak or shirt!
If nursing or with child, pray
It's not a sabbath or winter's day!
For then there will be great oppression
Such as there has never been.
If those days had not been shortened
Your flesh would no more be seen!
But they have indeed been shortened
For the sake of the elect.
If this claim of Christ's is important,
What does it mean? Was it correct?

One thing we can say for certain
Is that this cites *Daniel 9*,
And not the abomination of desolation
In Daniel 11 verse 31.
For that's the idol raised by Antiochus
At Jerusalem's holy site.
And that was in 167 BC —
Two hundred years before this night.
As the writer of this passage knew,
Daniel 9 predicts not this;
None of its seventieth 'week' was through
When Jesus warned of this distress.
And the next time an idol was installed
Upon Jerusalem's holy ground
Was when Hadrian placed a Roman god —
A statue — on the Temple mound.
And sure enough, there was oppression
From that day in all Judea:
Terrible war and forced expulsion
From their land in blood and fear.

But how long was this time of suffering
Originally meant to last?
The answer lies in Daniel 7
And our knowledge of the Past.
Although the eleventh horn is Vespasian
On the head of Rome's great beast,
That horn grows thicker and gets eyes in
And a mouth that makes great boasts.
Assuming the mouth is still Vespasian,
And its thickness many more kings,
The eyes can only be Emperor Hadrian —
The abomination is what he brings.
Hence the length of the oppression
Must be the time-phrase that comes next —
The "time, times and a half" expression
Until the kingdom's the elect's.
But what do those 'times' stand for there?
We can see from history.
It was a century and three quarters
Till Galerius' decree.

This means the 'times' are 'fifties',
For their ending has to come
When the elect became protected
By an emperor of Rome.
Although the same time-phrase appears
In Daniel 12, where they are years,
Its writer knew not what they meant
(As Daniel's incomprehension hints),
And predicting Antiochus seemed important –
Which may be why Christ said,
"They're shortened!".

Author's Note: The 'time, times and half a time' referred to in Daniel 7 is commonly claimed to mean 'three-and-a-half years'. For reasons that will be made clear in the next two poems, this is very unlikely to be the meaning intended by the person who first created the content of Daniel 7. Although it does appear to be the meaning attributed to this phrase by the writer of Daniel 12:11, this writer was writing around 165 BC (almost certainly long after the writer of Daniel 7). Moreover, judging from the fact that he portrays his character Daniel as *not being able to understand* this time phrase, it is reasonable to infer that he himself did not understand it either. Since his readers were likely to be equally ignorant of its meaning, I suspect he has taken the liberty of redefining it as 'three-and-a-half years'. That timescale suited his purpose of making a prophecy predicting an imminent end to the persecution that was ongoing in his day. Daniel 7, however, can only have been intended as a prediction of a *future* time of hardship that the 'holy people' would face long after that writer's day. And since the Jews had already endured times of hardship that were several *decades* in length, one should not expect it to be only three-and-a-half years. Each 'time' *must* be longer than a year, and should be a part of Jewish religion or culture. Given that the 'sevens' used in Daniel 9 are the 'seven-year-weeks' of Leviticus 25, it is extremely likely that those 'times' are the *'fifty-year' periods* specified in the same chapter of scripture, which makes the 'time, two times and half a time' a very respectable *175* years. It is therefore astonishing that this is the exact length of the time 136-311 AD when the Jews and Christians suffered persecution *and had no safe haven in the Holy Land.*

9. Hard Times

A year, they say, two more, and a half!
Go on! They must be having a laugh!
Did the worst hardship merely last
Till just three years and six months passed?

Perhaps. But history doesn't suggest
So few years would seem so bad.
As slaves in Egypt, they cried far longer
Till Moses came and made them glad.

And after Moses brought them out
They wandered homeless all about
The Sinai desert for *forty* years —
A very much longer time of tears.

And long after that, when Nebuchadnezzar
Destroyed the Temple of their God,
He brought them to old Babylon's river
Where, yay, they wept for *seventy* odd.

So perhaps those 'times' weren't meant to be
Years, but halves of a century —
The only times they had to keep
Exceeding Daniel's seven-year week.

Fifty years was the Jubilee
When slaves were meant to be set free —
A very obvious unit from heaven
For the persecution in Daniel 7.

A time, times and a half in length
Would then exceed all bad times past,
A century and three quarters last,
When the holy people had no strength.

And from the passage it must end
When Christianity's no more banned,
But free to thrive throughout the nation:
Galerius' Edict of Toleration.

So, when was this time begun?
From that edict in 311,
Going back a century and three fourths,
We reach 136 of course!

Wow! This best interpretation
Points to the expulsion from Judea —
The very moment the Jewish nation
Was homeless again for many a year!

And though one might suspect more options —
The starting point could be *before* —
The time from Hadrian's expulsions
Is when the Jews could fight no more.

And remember that both Jews and Christians
Are the holy people here,
So when the latter won protection,
In *God's* eyes, this trial was o'er.

Though persecutions did not cease,
God's people could still be at peace,
If they believed in the Son of Man,
Who in this passage ascends a throne.

It's astonishing that this simple phrase,
When interpreted the clearest way,
Exactly spans those fearful days
When Yahweh's people held no sway.

And it's even more of a surprise
That Hadrian, the king to whom applies
This handing over to the horn,
Is thus most probably its eyes!

For long before he set his sights
On rebuilding Jerusalem,
He travelled widely with his knights
To see the sights that called to him.

He was well-known for seeing it all.
Eyes are thus most suited
For the one to whom the Jews would fall
And out of Palestine be booted!

Author's Note: The fact that the 11th horn in Daniel 7 gains a *mouth* and *eyes* is quite astonishing when you consider that the two conquerors it must represent for the vision to be true are the *boastful* Vespasian and the *sightseeing* Hadrian.

10. A Jubilee Sandwich

Says Leviticus 25 verse 8:
Count *seven* Sevens of years.
To *forty-nine*, those Sevens equate,
And all these days are yours.

Then blast the trumpet! You shall keep
The fiftieth year for Me.
Emancipate, don't sow, nor reap,
And end all debts for free!

Some claim that this fiftieth year
Begins the following cycle.
They pretend the Sabbath is year one
(And the Son the angel Michael!).

"God wouldn't want adjacent years
When planting can't be done —
Folk too weak to hold their spears,
The rations all but gone!"

But what they rarely realise
Is that the point of this may be
To define a certain size of time
To measure history.

Says Leviticus 25 verse 3:
Sow and prune for six,
And in the seventh year stop for me
So the land can rest and fix.

This law appears to undermine
The Jubilee assumption,
That the cycle must be forty-nine
Years till its resumption.

If the seventh is a sabbath,
And the first a Jubilee,
One could but sow for five years,
However fit one be.

Hence, in order to not break that law,
Two sets of forty-nine
Must sandwich the Jubilee
Snugly in between.

Whilst that may not be thrifty,
And perhaps just done in heaven,
It makes one think of fifties
When assessing Daniel 7.

And only when we do that
Will its time prediction be
The era from the expulsion
Till *Galerius' decree!*

Since the ancient law of Moses
Has forced us to the view
That the times are likely fifty years
And not just one or two,

The fact that Jews and Christians
Did not rule a nation
For three-and-a-half fifties
Is a stunning observation;

For that's by far the only time
Consistent with the view
God's saints were given over to Rome,
Both Christian and Jew,

For a time, times and half a time,
As Daniel 7 states,
(Those kings of Rome the thickness
Of its horn anticipates).

And, of course, this means the Son of Man
That Daniel 7 describes
Must be Christ, and not that Michael
Who protects the twelve tribes.

But that is something history
Already hammers home:
It was the faith of *Christianity*
Which conquered that of Rome.

Author's Note: The 'Edict of Toleration' issued by the emperor Galerius in the Spring of 311 AD, which ended the Great Persecution of Christians, is by far the most obvious end of persecution prior to the Christian conquest of Rome in 312.

11. The Anointed One (Christ)

For your people and your holy city
seventy "weeks" are set,
To end sin and iniquity,
and atone for the debt;
For righteousness eternal
to be welcomed — That's the point! —
To seal up vision and prophecy,
and the Holiest *anoint*.

There'll be seven "weeks" and sixty-two
from when the word goes out
To build Jerusalem anew
until *Anointed One*'s about —
A king for whom it will again
be built in times distraught.
After the sixty-two is when
that Christ is killed, with nought.

'Anointed One' is 'Christ' in Greek,
and 'Holiest' is thought
To be the Temple's inner sanctum —
though here it's clearly not,
For the Anointed One's a *king*
who dies, with nothing to his name.
Since the Holiest gets *anointed*,
we should conclude he is the same!

This means the seven "sevens"
(or 'weeks' where each day is a year)
And the sixty-two "sevens"
(in years: four hundred and thirty-four)
Can't both end with Anointed One
(since no-one can survive
For over four centuries
and still be quite alive);

Which means those seven "sevens"
and the sixty-two are joined —
If they were separate or overlapped,
the former would not point
To any hopes or fears
that this passage does envision.
So, it's *sixty-nine times seven years*
to Christ, from The Permission.

But the 'years', here, within each 'seven'
needn't mean 'calendar cycles'.
Although their meaning is not yet known,
'twelve months' is fairly likely —
But it's probably the repeating unit
that both the times involve
In Daniel 12:11
and Daniel 12:12.

The twelve hundred and ninety days
the former verse provided —
Three-and-a-half 360s
with a month of thirty added —
Is the thirteen hundred and thirty-five —
the latter verse's score —
less the month-and-a-half it took
the Temple to restore.

The year-like unit in both of these —
three hundred and sixty days —
Makes the sixty-nine seven-year weeks
Four hundred and seventy-six
Solar years, and twenty-four days,
And two thirds, to be precise.
Incredibly, this length of time
fits the facts real nice!

The time the word went out
to rebuild Jerusalem
Was when Nehemiah set about
to restore his people's home —
His permission from the Persian king
in 444 BC (early March).
Adding the sixty-nine 'sevens' gives
AD 33 (late March).

The latter is at least
the most probable year
For the crucifixion of Jesus Christ —
the Christ who did appear
At the gates of Jerusalem
in late March 33,
When as "King!" he's hailed,
and later nailed naked to a tree.

Even the extra sixteen hours
was probably required.
For Christ rode in triumphantly,
looked round, and then retired;
It was late afternoon alright,
whilst Nehemiah would
Approach his master late at night
on a day that had been good.

Whatever you may think
about the 'sevens' in this dream,
What shouldn't be in doubt
is the starting point I claim.
For the prayer in Daniel 9
to which this prophecy's appended,
Is derived from Nehemiah's
after which his wish was granted!

Why would a writer attach
a prayer so derived
To this contextual match,
unless he firmly believed
The word to build Jerusalem,
of which this passage speaks,
Was the one Nehemiah held
when gathering his bricks?

And the sixty-nine 'weeks'
couldn't then have ended
Before the first century,
as scholars have demanded,
For the wall that Nehemiah built
would constantly remind
The citizens of Jerusalem
of the "weeks" that were behind!

Author's Note: The fact that the prophecy in Daniel 9 clearly specifies a *sixty-nine seven-year-week time interval* from the permission to rebuild Jerusalem (the one given to Nehemiah, as the prayer before it indicates) to the arrival of a Christ who would 'be king' and 'get killed emptyhanded' is astonishing in itself. However, the discovery that this prediction is likely to be perfectly accurate when the years are all 360 days long is mind-blowing. That is because 360 days is not just any old year-length. Calendar cycles in ancient times tended to be shorter than this, being usually based on months measured by the phase-cycles of the moon. But most years were still *twelve calendar months*, and months were usually *thirty days*, making it very reasonable to think of a year as *360 days*. Crucially, there is evidence of this in Daniel 12:11-12. What makes this fulfilment really surprising is that a carpenter like Christ had little hope of working out when to arrive in order to *deliberately* fulfil such a time period.

12. The End Determined

As Hadrian lay dying
In his villa by the sea,
He knew not that his passing
Would fulfil a prophecy —

A prediction so precise
Its fulfilment is proof
That Jesus is the kingly Christ,
And Daniel 9 the truth:

After two and sixty "sevens"
That its seven "sevens" precede,
A Christ the king will be 'cut off',
And nothing by him be had,

The people of a *coming* king
Will wreck God's house and city.
But *his* end, a terrible flood will bring —
All-out war. No pity.

War won't sleep until the end
And there'll be desolation.
That king will keep a covenant
For a seven-year duration.

A promise made to many,
For a "week" he will confirm,
Until the end that is decreed
Is poured out onto *him*.

In the middle of those seven years
He'll cause the cessation
Of sacrifice and offering —
The customary oblation —

And upon a "wing" or "overspreading",
Raise an abomination —
The idol Jews were dreading:
Their ultimate desolation.

Notice that the end decreed
Is that poured on this king.
His death concludes the seventieth "week" —
His deeds upon that "wing".

But what begins that seventieth "week"?
The confirming of a vow
That many will hear him speak,
And the context lets us know:

It says, "this king's *people*
Will destroy (and thus *bring down*)
The city and the temple";
Suggesting he'll not be around

When Jerusalem is first destroyed
After Christ is killed.
This means his vow ought to be
A promise to *rebuild*.

That destruction was its sack by Rome
In 70 AD.
The next Roman king to come
Was Hadrian, you see.

Who promised to rebuild it all
When he arrived in state;
And kept that promise right until
His death in 138!

Since he came in late 130
(An inscription reveals),
And travelled south to party —
Where death his lover steals —

The building must have started
In the summer of 131.
So, he and this world parted
Not a moment too soon.

And not a moment too late,
For he died within July —
Seven years from the best date
For that founding ceremony.

And amazingly,
Amidst those seven years, it's true,
He caused the sacrifice to cease,
Never to be renewed,

By crushing a rebellion,
And expelling all the Jews
From Jerusalem and much
Of the land that once was theirs.

He's remembered still
For ploughing — *overspreading* — the city
And establishing an idol
On the mount that once was pretty.

The 'beautiful mountain'
Where the Temple had once stood
Gained a statue of Hadrian,
And a shrine unto his god.

He renamed Jerusalem
'Aelia Capitolina',
And the ancient Jewish homeland
'Syria Palestina'.

His family name was Aelius,
And Capitoline the home
Of the idol on the overspreading —
The foremost god of Rome.

And around the time of this, you'll find,
Hadrian became ill.
For two whole years, his health declined
Till eventually he lay still —

Exactly seven years of blood
From his founding of this city,
Which had brought about that awful flood:
That conflict without pity.

Author's Note: The fact that Hadrian died *seven years after he re-founded Jerusalem* is stunning! It perfectly fulfilled the 'Ruler who will come' prediction in Daniel 9. Although that prophecy does not explicitly say that the promise this ruler would fulfil for seven years was to be the rebuilding of Jerusalem, that is surely what it implies. It is, after all, stated to be about Daniel's people and city, and in the previous verse it predicts that city's destruction. Having told us that 'the people of the ruler who will come will destroy the city and the sanctuary' sometime after the death of a Christ in the first half of the first century AD, it then tells us that 'his (or its) end will come with a flood' (a commonly used metaphor for a full-scale war), and that 'war will go on until the end'. The ruler who will come is thus indicated to be a ruler of the same people who will destroy Jerusalem and the Temple (but presumably not the leader of these people at that time, or it would have omitted the words 'the people of'). Since Jerusalem and the Temple were destroyed by the *Romans* in 70 AD, the prophecy predicts that a *Roman* ruler will come to the site of Jerusalem and confirm a public promise to rebuild that city *for a seven-year period ending with his death*. We know that this is precisely what Hadrian did! Since he visited Jerusalem in 130, the building work probably began (after preparations) in 131; and he died in 138. That is already amazingly accurate, but the prophecy doesn't end there. It also tells us that in the middle of those seven years this ruler would 'put a stop to sacrifice and offering', and 'on an overspreading raise an abomination of desolation' (a foreign idol) that would remain in place at least until his death. We know from history and archaeology that this is also exactly what Hadrian did. It is not widely appreciated, but the destruction of the Second Temple in 70 AD did not stop the Jews making sacrifices and offerings at the Temple site. That was only stopped when Hadrian secured Jerusalem (in 134) and later exiled the Jews from it following his crushing victory over Bar Kochba and their second revolt in 135. He then had a shrine and statue erected on the Temple Mount. Intriguingly, the revolt had been caused in part by his having that holy site *ploughed over* in preparation for his building work – a ploughing over that is depicted on Roman coins found in caves occupied by the Jewish rebels, and which would be very reasonably described as an 'overspreading'!

After the city of Aelia was established upon the ruins of Jerusalem,
Aelius Hadrian vanquished the rebelling Jews
in their conflict with the general, Timus [Tineius] Rufus.
It was at that time that the sacrifice and offering ceased
and will continue to cease even unto the completion of the age,
and the desolation is going to endure until the very end.

St Jerome

(Commentary on Daniel, ca. 407 AD, my emphasis)

PART THREE

PEOPLE AND PLACES

13. The Dying Hadrian's Address to his Soul

Ah soul, sweet soul,
So hard to pin down,
So little of me,
Yet so precious you've grown —
Guest of my body,
Which served you so well
As beloved best friend,
As palatial hotel.
To where will you go
When at last you check out —
Leaving comforts you know
For the strangeness without:
The paleness and stiffness
And bareness beyond,
No brain to provide
Things of which you are fond?
Beauty and grace
And variety bereft,
Your usual enjoyments,
They all must be left.

14. Nehemiah's Defence

In Nisan of your twentieth year
(I count them from Tishri),
I received the wine as usual
and offered it to thee.
I hadn't looked so sad before,
and so you asked me why.
Naturally I was afraid —
afraid that I would die.

"May you live for ever!", I said,
"Why shouldn't I be sad?
When the city of my fathers' tombs
lies waste, I can't be glad.
Its gates have been consumed by fire,
its walls are broken down."
You answered, "What do you desire?"
I knelt upon the ground.

I prayed to God, and said to thee,
"If it pleases you my king,
If I've found favour in your sight,
then grant me just one thing:
Send me where my fathers lie.
Please grant me this in pity!
Send me to the land of Judah
with the right to build that city."

You asked how long I'd be away
(The queen was by your side).
I set a time. You said "Okay".
There was nothing I did hide.
You gave me letters to the lords
of the lands beyond the river
That I may safely cross their wards
until I come to Judah.

You even gave me a letter
for the keeper of the forests,
Demanding from him timber
to replace the ruined doorposts
Of the citadel by the temple,
and for the house where I would stay.
I thanked you for these gracious gifts,
and you blessed me on my way.

Those lords are lying when they say
that I have gone beyond my call.
They're merely trying to delay
the completion of my wall.
They are not doing this for thee,
as I'm sure you can tell.
With Judah no longer weak, they fear
they can never more rebel.

My people owe too much to you
to not do what you say.
This wall will only ever keep
your enemies at bay.
Only one thing is correct
about the documents they cite.
King Cyrus *didn't* permit this act.
It's to *you* we owe this right!

Jerusalem is a city again
because of what you said.
My people will remember this
long after I am dead.
Whenever they look upon this wall
and assess how long it's stood,
They and my God will think of you,
and bless you for this good!

Author's Note: The royal permission to rebuild Jerusalem that Nehemiah receives in Nehemiah 2:1-8 simply has to be 'the word to restore and rebuild Jerusalem' that the prophecy in Daniel 9:25 refers to. That is because the prayer immediately preceding this prophecy (Daniel 9:4-19) is so similar to the prayer Nehemiah prays prior to receiving this permission (Nehemiah 1:5-11) that the former is almost certainly *derived* from the latter. And if that is the case, the book's compiler has to have had that very permission on his mind when he attached the prophecy. It is in any case by far the most obvious 'word to restore and rebuild Jerusalem' that the Old Testament contains. From its issuance in early March 444 BC, it was exactly 69×7×360 days (69 'weeks of years') until late March 33 AD, which is by far the most likely date for the Triumphal Entry and subsequent crucifixion of Jesus Christ (the most famous 'anointed one' in history). Since years are 360 days in Dan. 12:11, the prophecy was exactly right!

15. The Clock

The wall Nehemiah erected
Is a clock that, for years,
was protected.
So that those who incline
To squeeze Daniel 9
Can with ease, for all time,
be rejected.

16. Vespasian

The problem with assuming Daniel was written as it claims,
At, or shortly after, the time of the royals whom it names,
Is that this would mean accepting a prediction was made,
In which subsequent history is correctly portrayed.

But even if one opts to trust the latest date suggested —
Four hundred years after, in peace, king Nebuchadnezzar rested —
One's still faced with a true account of history in advance —
A mistaken view of the past that matched the future just by chance?

In Babylon, in the first year of Belshazzar the king,
Daniel had a vivid dream — a very unusual thing.
He wrote down the substance of that vision when it ceased,
And it portrays the next *nine* centuries of history in the East.

He dreamt of four enormous beasts that rose up from the sea —
Each different from the others, and arising separately —
The first was like a lion, with eagle's wings to beat.
The second a leaning bear. It was told to rise and eat.

The third — like a leopard — had four birdlike wings,
It also had four heads, and gained the authority of kings.
Yet after it, a fourth appeared, with dreadful crushing power.
With large iron teeth, it broke the things it would devour.

It was different from the other beasts, and trampled underneath
What was left of its victims after it crushed them with its teeth.
And this beast had ten horns — but Daniel then goes on to say,
There grew an eleventh horn, and three were plucked up from its way.

That horn gained human eyes, and a mouth as it grew higher.
Daniel watched that beast get slain, and consumed by God's own fire.
He then saw one like a son of man come with clouds of heaven,
To whom worship by all nations and unending power was given.

In his dream, Daniel asked what meaning to this applies.
He was told, the four enormous beasts are kingdoms that will rise.
The last will differ from the rest, and crush the entire earth.
The ten horns are ten kings who, from it, will come forth.

After them, another king, unlike them, will arise.
He'll put down three of the former ten, to take the throne they prize.
He'll speak against the Most High, whose saints he will oppress,
Until a court rules in their favour, and the kingdom they possess.

What's cool about this vision is that the features of each beast
Recall those of one of the empires that, from that time, ruled the East.
The first is clearly Babylon, as it loses its great wings,
Reminding us of Daniel 4, and the greatest of her kings.

The second must be the empire of the Medes and the Persians —
With a higher side (the Persians) and an appetite for invasions,
It swallowed up many lands, including Babylon's estate —
And the third the Greek empire of Alexander the Great.

The swiftness of a leopard suggests how fast the East was won,
And its four heads the four Greek dynasties who rose up when he'd gone.
The four wings are the four parts into which that empire split
When Alexander the Great had died and his generals divided it.

The fourth beast should then portray the empire that defeated
Those kingdoms of the Greeks (ere Daniel was completed).
That, of course, was Rome, with its highly trained legions,
Which crushed all opposition in those Middle Eastern regions.

If those legions are the iron teeth, then what might be the horns?
Taking 'kings' to mean 'sole rulers that unlimited reign adorns',
The first is Sulla, then Julius Caesar, Augustus and Tiberius,
Caligula, Claudius, Nero, Galba, Otho and Vitellius.

Then what about the eleventh horn foretold in Daniel's vision?
It can only be the next emperor, Flavius Vespasian.
Fittingly, Vespasian was indeed unlike the ten —
His father wasn't in the Senate (Rome's leading men).

Spookily, as predicted, the very year he came to power
Three other Roman emperors met their final hour:
On 15th January 69, Otho had Galba killed;
But slew himself, on 16th April, when Vitellius won the field.

In late December of that same year, troops loyal to Vespasian
Entered Rome and killed Vitellius, as he attempted to evade them,
Vespasian was made emperor by the Senate he barely suited,
Fulfilling the vision of the small horn before which were three uprooted.

Vespasian was also boastful like that small horn Daniel saw —
Publishing great omens, to fill his folk with awe,
Claiming a Jewish prophecy, to gain acceptance from abroad,
And on his deathbed saying, "Oh my, I must be becoming a god!"

Another feature of Vespasian that fits with Daniel's vision
Is that in AD 66, by Nero's decision,
He was granted a command to stop a rebellion in Judea,
And set out with sixty thousand troops early the next year.

He swiftly conquered Galilee, as one the Jews would fear,
And planned the siege of Jerusalem, bringing its devastation near.
In AD 69, he went to fight against Vitellius,
Leaving it to his son to crush the Jews who were rebellious.

In the summer of AD 70, with Vespasian's throne secured,
Jerusalem fell to the Romans, and its destruction was assured.
They burned down the Temple, making it difficult for the Jews
To hold their annual feasts and keep the requirements of their laws.

Thus Vespasian fought the Jews, like the eleventh horn Daniel saw,
And may have had their temple burned to stop them keeping their law.
But this was two whole centuries after the latest Daniel's dated
(In the reign of the "mad" Epiphanes, whose evil deeds it slated)!

And of course, its claim that later on a certain Jewish sect
Would rule the Roman Empire also proved correct.
But the really astonishing detail this vision did foretell
Is that the eleventh emperor-king of Rome would three before him fell.

Although Vespasian, himself, remained safely in the East,
When Galba was assassinated and Otho was deceased,
Tacitus makes it clear he had supporters back in Rome
Whom Otho rewarded generously when Galba was dethroned.

And it's firmly within reason to suspect that these supporters
Encouraged Otho to wage war against his rival in the north.
One rival would thus be removed, and another greatly weakened.
And the backers of the former, to Vespasian, would stream forth.

Josephus, whom he captures, and amazingly befriends
Has his captor, around that time, judge such actions by their ends:
"Those who shine in combat, no greater kudos warrant
Than those who accomplish just as much by intelligence and restraint!"

Thus it's likely that Vespasian did indeed subdue all three,
Making Daniel 7 even *more* astonishing to see.
But whether that's true or not, the uprooting of three horns
Is incredibly symbolic of how his emperorship was born.

No such thing happened when Epiphanes seized his throne.
Although he slew a usurper, and a boy with no crown,
And took the place of another who was far away in Rome,
The latter wouldn't have seemed a king to anyone at the time.

And if an uncrowned infant were really given a horn
Much bigger than one that Epiphanes were given,
Size would have to stand for the legality of a king
And a usurper ought to have by far the *tiniest* wee thing!

But *even if* some seemingly blind Seleucid defender
Saw his empire as a *distinct kind*, and *stronger than Alexander*,
And believed that this usurper had a rightful royal claim,
It would still be strange Rome's future turned out to be "the same!"

17. Josephus' Insistence on Rome

If Daniel's fourth empire were Greece,
Josephus risked nothing but peace,
If he'd said that the horn,
Before which three were torn,
Was the king Laenas ordered to cease!

Author's Note: In *the Year of the Four Emperors* (69 AD) the Roman general Vespasian, of relatively humble upbringing, became the eleventh dictator to be given an unlimited reign over the Roman Empire (the first was Sulla and the second Julius Caesar). Since his supporters in Rome almost certainly caused the downfall of the three previous emperors (Galba, Otho and Vitellius) in order to get him there, his rise to power perfectly fulfilled the prediction in Daniel 7 that the eleventh king would be different from the previous ten and would subdue three of them. Moreover, since his army was in the process of conquering the Jews at the time, the prediction that this king would 'defeat the holy people' was also perfectly fulfilled. The first-century Jewish historian Josephus was captured by that army in 67 AD after the city he was tasked with defending had fallen. Unusually, his life was spared when he prophesied that Vespasian would become emperor. As a prisoner in the Roman camp, he befriended the future emperor Titus. And after Vespasian took the throne, he was released from captivity, honoured and encouraged to write about his experiences (no doubt as part of the propaganda machine that Vespasian felt necessary to secure his family's grip on power). He immediately wrote a detailed account of the Jewish revolt (*The Jewish War*), which provides historians with a wealth of information about Jewish society prior to the destruction of the First Temple in Vespasian's first full year as emperor. And it also describes the Roman battle tactics and introduces you to Vespasian himself in the crucial years before he became the eleventh dictator to be vested with an unlimited reign over the Roman Empire. Later in life (around 93 AD) he also completed his other great historical work (*Antiquities of the Jews*) in which he wrote in detail about the book of Daniel. Unlike the later Christian commentators, Josephus had absolutely *no incentive* to interpret the fourth empire in Daniel 7 as Rome. This was liable to get him into serious trouble with his patrons. If the Jews had ever thought it was Greece and Antiochus Epiphanes, he would have said so. Yet he makes it clear (through his detailed account of Daniel 2) that it is Rome. The fact that he only alludes to Daniel 7, rather than covering it in detail, even suggests that he thought it predicted Vespasian. The critical consensus on this passage is thus indefensible.

18. Darius the Mede

He captured ancient Babylon
at the age of sixty-two;
Succeeded Belshazzar,
whom, apparently, he slew;
Was made king of that city
For just a year or two;
And appointed local governors
to tax the kingdom through.

A hundred and twenty governors,
he thought the right amount;
And appointed three presidents
to whom they would account.
His favourite was Daniel,
who never did miscount.
He planned to set him over them,
which none of them did want.

He signed a royal edict
that those governors had written
Promising the lions' den
for anyone who'd petition
Anyone else for thirty days
except his royal person.
(It was going to be a busy month.
That was for certain!).

When Daniel was brought to him
for breaking his decree,
He laboured intensively
all day to set him free.
He was extremely unhappy
he'd been tricked in such a way;
But concluded, rather strangely,
"What I've written has to stay!"

He allowed his men to lecture him
in a patronising tone:
Reminding him of what he'd signed,
and what this Daniel 'd done;
Telling him that *his decree*
could never be undone —
The law of the Medes *and Persians*
must be left alone!

He reluctantly cast Daniel
into the lions' den,
Saying, "May God deliver you!"
and sealing it with a stone.
He spent the night in turmoil,
all sleep and pleasures gone,
And ran back very early
to open up the den.

As he neared, he called in anguish,
"Daniel! You alive?
Were you delivered from the lions
by the God you always serve?"
Relieved, he heard his Daniel say,
"My king, forever live!
God's angel shut the lions' mouths,
for no sin did I have!"

In joy, he brought this Daniel out,
and threw his accusers in.
Them, their wives, their children too,
were all found to be with sin!
For the lions mauled and ripped them up,
and broke their every bone,
Before they even hit the floor
of that wicked little den!

Though surely propaganda,
this story does reveal
That this unknown king Darius
may in fact be real.
For the man who captured Babylon
when to Persia it fell,
Governed part of Media,
and then Babylon as well.

He also chose governors,
and died within two years —
When this kingship passed to Cyrus,
whom this Mede no doubt fears.
The overlordship of Cyrus,
this passage calls to mind,
For why else would this Darius *fear*
to break the law he'd signed?

The importance of this passage, though,
is that many now declare,
"This Darius was invented
to make Media the bear!"
He certainly does no such thing —
a *Persian* king he was —
A puppet ruler, afraid to alter
Medo-*Persian* laws.

Author's Note: The mainstream view that Darius the Mede was invented by the writer of the book of Daniel in order to make the four-kingdoms prophecy point to the 160s BC seems to me to be indefensible. If that had been the intention, the writer would surely have had him ruling according to *'the law of the Medes'* rather than *'the law of the Medes and Persians'*. The latter clearly implies that he is a king of the *Medo-Persian empire* (or at least the part of it constituting the kingdom of Babylon as the text indicates) – the same empire represented by the ram in Daniel 8. Moreover, he is clearly not the emperor or the chief authority over that empire. If he were, he would not have been in the least bit afraid to cancel the decree he had been tricked into signing. Although history is silent about this character (just as it once was about king Belshazzar of Daniel 5), his actions strongly imply that he was the general Ugbaru (or Gubaru) – governor of Gutium (Media) – who took Babylon for Cyrus. In fact, there is evidence that Cyrus was *not* known as 'King of Babylon' until a year or two after that event.

Porphyry assigned the last two beasts,
that of the Macedonians and that of the Romans,
to the one realm of the Macedonians
and divided them up as follows.
He claimed that the leopard was Alexander himself,
and that the beast which was dissimilar to the others
represented the four successors of Alexander,
and then he enumerates ten kings up to the time of Antiochus,
surnamed Epiphanes, and who were very cruel.
And he did not assign the kings themselves to separate kingdoms,
for example Macedon, Syria, Asia, or Egypt,
but rather he made the various kingdoms a single realm
consisting of a series.
This he did of course in order that the words which were written:
"…a mouth uttering overweening boasts"
might be considered as spoken about Antiochus…

St Jerome

(Commentary on Daniel, ca. 407 AD)

PART FOUR

HYPOTHESES

19. The Document

Commander, I have prepared
the document requested.
Morale is low, the people are scared,
their faith is sorely tested.
It's high time for this small deception —
All else has been tried!
We must be bold in its reception, though.
They cannot think we've lied!

I've written the final prophecy,
and attached the stories too,
And linked them to the real predictions
for those who may see through.
I've also written another
to go earlier in the book —
So that the 'four monsters' vision
can't be overlooked.

Inspired by the bear and leopard,
I wrote of two more beasts —
A dream portraying Alexander's
conquest of the East,
His empire splitting into four,
and Epiphanes arising —
Don't worry, I used horns —
not heads — for the dividing!

My use of only *two* beasts
for this prophecy of our time,
Will mean they cannot miss the fact
that the fourth before is Rome.
I've even named them 'Medo-Persia'
and 'Greece', for safety's sake!
They'd have to be incredibly thick
to make such a mistake!

Obviously, we cannot make it
any *more* transparent.
If we're seeking the Senate's help,
we can't risk it being apparent
That this prophecy predicts
the fall of Rome in time to come —
To our people, after she destroys
all Jerusalem!

And I've also added a prayer
to the vision of the "sevens".
Since its evil king does much the same
as Antiochus, I think they'll claim
The starting point was much before
Nehemiah went out his door
To build anew the city wall
and make our men again stand tall.

So, I've made our Daniel pray
a prayer to remind them of that day
When Nehemiah prayed his prayer
and gained his permission to repair.
But don't worry, I've made my prayer much longer!
None will recognise it as his.
It's repetitive, and a great deal stronger,
than the one that he prayed is.

So, I think we're ready for battle
to win the minds of our people back!
The Greeks have slaughtered them like cattle.
We must provide the faith they lack!
I know it may seem like lying,
but it's war in which we act!
When Joshua sent our people spying
deceptiveness he did expect!

In fact, I've thought a lot about it.
Didn't alter prophecies that were real —
Even leaving some in Aramaic.
So, if from God, they'll still not fail.
And we've truthfully attributed them to Daniel.
We've even evidenced a date.
So, when people see events unfolding
they'll *know* they're real, and God is great!

20. Persia (Paarsa)

In Old Persian 'protected' was 'pa-'
And 'brave animal' or 'bear' was 'arsa'.
So, did Jews infer
That 'protected by bear'
Was the most likely meaning of 'Paarsa'?

21. Porphyry's View of the Leopard

Some scholars of Daniel do say
That Porphyry showed them the way.
But that isn't true,
Because Porphyry's view,
Is *not* the consensus today.

22. The Critical Consensus

In scholarship there is a view
that is quite unjustifiable —
That all claims of real prediction
in Daniel are deniable,
Unless they place events
around the 160s BC.
Anything that seems later,
scholars assume it cannot be.

This assumption isn't justified,
for the writer had good reason
To have prophecies that applied
to a distant future season.
They'd be there to stop the skeptics
who would otherwise say,
"All the visions are fulfilled.
I think it was written the other day!"

But they make that assumption
regardless of this fact.
Any prediction that appears to be
about a future act,
Long after the deeds
of the Seleucid kings,
Is nevertheless assumed to be
about those very things!

Daniel 7, for illustration,
says an eleventh king will rise,
Who'll subdue three of his nation
and wage war upon the Jews.
Scholars immediately assume
that this is Antiochus the Fourth,
The Seleucid king by whom
many Jews were put to death.

But this requires that the empire
this eleventh monarch ruled
Be identified as Greece
(or what the Seleucids controlled),
And the one that came before it
(the leopard, not the bear)
Be identified as Persia
even though it has four heads!

They thus forget that people everywhere,
for many centuries,
Saw the *bear* as Medo-Persia
and the leopard as *Greece*,
Because the latter has 'four heads' (and wings)
and the former 'one side higher',
And *Greek* rule split in four
and crushed a *Persian*-ruled empire.

And that Persian-ruled empire
was a known continuation
Of a Median dynasty
by a Persian usurpation —
As represented in Daniel 8
by a higher and lower share
Of a single beast (a ram),
just like the sides of Daniel's *bear*.

Instead, they claim that bear to be
Media — that's all! —
A mistaken view of history,
for Babylon did fall
To the *Persian*-ruled empire
(the *leopard*, they infer!),
And Babylon was the Lion,
after which appeared *that bear*.

Their view makes a nonsense
of the features of the beasts,
Which they admit are then 'obscure',
or ambiguous at best,
And nothing that a reader would think
uniquely characterises
The empires that those scholars claim
each beast symbolises.

The reasoning they use
is that the king in Daniel 7
Makes war upon the Jews,
and to him that nation's given.
But such a war would surely be
common to Jewish prophecy —
A plausible prediction
that would stop the skeptics dead.

In fact, the writer of this book
had a very strong incentive
To make his real predictions look
somewhat like the present is.
Such likenesses would stimulate
his readers to investigate,
And they would thereby find
that those events were not behind!

Hence the *timing* must come first
and not the nature of events
In deciding what each prophecy
most probably represents.
Only when we ascertain
what readers would think of that
Can we say which are predictions,
and which are likely not.

They'd easily see the leopard
in Daniel's dream as *Greece* —
Just as Porphyry and Josephus did.
Its four heads scream of this!
Since the empire of that eleventh king
is totally unique,
And comes after that of the leopard,
we can be sure he isn't Greek!

In fact, as Rome's hold
upon the Seleucid crown
Was twenty-five years old —
and not, by any means, unknown
At the time the final piece
of the book of Daniel's written —
We should assume that *Rome's* that final beast,
the eleventh king a prediction.

And the same, in fact, applies
to the king in Daniel 9,
Who in several different ways
seems like Antiochus again.
But not when you do the sums
and work out just how long
After Nehemiah, he comes —
That tells you, you are wrong!

Even if you started
from the date of the vision,
You're still long after Antiochus'
hated decision
To attack Jerusalem,
and the sacrifice to end.
But why should that not be
what the writer did intend?

Those claiming this was Antiochus
would all be left in doubt
When history was explained to them,
and this was pointed out;
Which is a plausible reason
for this passage to be added —
Another vision of Antiochus
was hardly something needed!

Hence, because real predictions
would be useful in this book,
And those that seemed like known events
felt to be worth a look,
One shouldn't assume such prophecies,
which it clearly does include,
Were *not* meant as predictions —
and as predictions *understood*.

23. The Historical Preparation

If a God exists who wished to reveal to humankind
A message not easy to dismiss as humanly designed,
Nor easily overlooked among such false revelations,
We'd expect that God to make for it substantial preparations.

For by making delivery difficult, and announced in advance,
He'd surprise us into giving it more than just a glance,
And at the same time prevent us being persuaded by the claim,
The messenger wasn't from God — just a human seeking fame.

Of all religious messages, the hardest to deliver
Was the message of Jesus Christ, who said he had to be handed over
To suffer under enemies, and then be crucified,
And rise again to life the third day after he had died.

Apart from fear of suffering, there are several reasons why
The delivery of such a message would be hard for you or I:
As folk don't normally resurrect, I'd have to stop me dying,
And do so in a secret way, so none would catch me lying.

But the requirement that my enemies be the ones to execute me
Means I can't control what happens — whether they hang or beat or shoot me.
Furthermore, it's unlikely I could *secretly* cheat death.
Enemies would be keen to ensure that I draw no more breath!

But the hardest requirement of Christ's teaching wasn't his resurrection,
But the fact that he had to be *free from sin* when killed by crucifixion.
There had to be no hint of lies or hate in his career,
He had to have always loved his neighbour and kept his conscience clear.

This alone makes that teaching more likely than any other
To be a message from a Creator God (whom Jesus called his Father).
But there's even more evidence that's supportive of this claim,
For the messenger's life seems to have been foretold before he came.

An account of such a messenger was already written down
Long before Christ's birth in a book his followers would have known.
In view of this, he had be seen to do what was predicted,
And couldn't have changed his ways whenever a circumstance conflicted.

Centuries before Christ, Isaiah prophesied,
Speaking about a servant who suffered like Christ and died,
"Who has believed our message; to whom has God's arm been revealed?
He grew up like a tender shoot — a root in a parched field.

He had no beauty or majesty that would attract us to him —
Nothing in his appearance that would make us wish we knew him.
He was despised and rejected — enduring suffering a lot —
Like one men hide their faces from, shunned and valued not.

He surely shouldered our discomforts, and our own sorrows bore.
Yet we considered him stricken by God, and smitten by him so sore.
But he was pierced for our transgressions, and for our sins was killed.
He paid the price that brought us peace, and by his wounds we're healed.

By oppression and judgement he was taken away,
And of his descendants, who can say?
He was cut off from the land that the living know
For the sins of my people who were due the blow.

It was the Lord's will to crush him, and bring upon him suffering.
And though the Lord makes his life a guilt offering,
He will see his offspring and prolong his days,
And the Lord's will shall prosper in his hands always.

After the suffering of his soul, he'll see the light and be satisfied.
By my righteous servant's knowledge, many will be justified....
He was numbered with the sinners, and bore their transgression,
And for all the transgressors, he himself made intercession."

Elsewhere in Isaiah's book, his God makes very clear
He isn't meaning someone past or someone standing near:
"See, the former things have happened, and I declare things new.
Before they spring to being I'm announcing them to you!"

Intriguingly, there's evidence that suggests this may be true.
The source is the book of Daniel — another prophetic Jew —
A resident of Babylon in 553 BC,
Where the Jews were living in exile, longing to be free.

That evidence is a prophecy that might not date much later —
Archaeology has confirmed details noted by the writer
That aren't found in subsequent historical documentation
(Such as a king called Belshazzar, and his political situation).

But whenever it was written, it was definitely before
The events that it predicts, which are predicted very clear.
We know that this is true for it came to be employed
To authenticise a famous book where history is portrayed.

And copies of that ancient book were found at Qumran —
Buried in haste shortly ere the Romans overran
The whole of Judea, under a man who'd rise to fame
For succeeding three emperors who had a better claim.

This unique event, amazingly, this strange book did foresee.
The eleventh king of the Roman world, it says, will topple three.
He'll fight against God's people, who will subsequently fall,
And it even says that later on their faith will conquer all.

In fact, it is the faith of folk who worship a *Son* —
Depicted as being led to God and seated on a throne —
That faith, which is to *fill the world*, after Rome is won
Only therefore applies to the faith that *Christ* began.

And astonishingly, another passage found within that book,
When interpreted the way the text most clearly justifies,
Predicts the time, to within a month, for all who care to look,
Of the arrival of this Christ at the city where he dies!

And also the destruction of Jerusalem by Rome,
And the timing of the death of an emperor to come,
Who would end Jewish sacrifice and raise an abomination
On a famous overspreading — Hadrian's desecration.

So it seems the book of Daniel has been carefully prepared
For those who need objective proof the message of Christ was shared
By a being who can engineer the fulfilment of predictions
That humans would have no chance of fulfilling by their actions.

But let's not become *obsessed* with that careful preparation.
What matters is the message and what we do with the information.
Christ said, *"You think by learning scripture, eternal life you'll earn.*
But the scriptures speak of me, and yet to me you do not turn."

24. The Rock

The stone that was rejected,
Quarried without hands
From the mountain of Moses,
Crushes all on whom it lands.

That capstone God has taken
Has become a giant hill,
Where those who fall are broken,
And which keeps on rising still.

That hill is now a mountain.
It's the kingdom of the Christ.
It fills, like a fountain,
Every nation of the earth.

That mountain is a people
Who adore a Son of Man —
Their faith replaced Rome's
And every nation overran.

And that faith had its founding
When the Empire phase began.
But its progress wasn't astounding
Ere the Jews would lose their land.

Its conquest was accomplished
In spite of great oppression —
A century and three quarters,
With no haven from aggression.

And amazingly, this was foretold
In Daniel 7 and 2 —
Even the years that would unfold
From the expulsion of the Jews.

Yet even that is imprecise
Compared to Daniel 9.
Its timing of the Holy Christ
Can only be divine!

So let's accept Christ's God as real —
Our doubts reject for Pascal's deal.
And let's elect to help and heal,
Acknowledge Christ, and to him kneel.

For in doing so we will ensure
That after death we'll still endure
To praise again the one who'll save us
From an eternity that would enslave us.

Author's Note: The seventeenth century French mathematician Blaise Pascal argued that it is more rational to believe than to doubt God's existence because if you believe and happen to be wrong you lose nothing, whereas if you don't believe and happen to be wrong you risk eternal hell. Whilst the concept of hell doesn't seem consistent with a righteous God or science, scientists don't actually know what your consciousness is. So those who claim that at death it ceases to exist are speaking from ignorance. One thing they are right about, though, is that without the input from a brain we cannot expect to have experiences that contain wonderful information. Any experience we have will be vastly impoverished. We won't know what anything is. To me, that's hell, and is quite probable. The accuracy of Daniel 7 and 9 suggests it may only be avoided by following Christ.

APPENDIX

ANNOTATED BIBLE TEXTS

The Statue Dream (Daniel 2:31-45)

[31]"You, O king, saw, and behold, a great image. This image, which was mighty, and whose brightness was excellent, stood before you; and its appearance was terrifying. [32]As for this image, its head was of fine gold, its breast and its arms of silver, its belly and its thighs of bronze, [33]its legs of iron, its feet part of iron, and part of clay. [34]You saw until a stone was cut out ['of a mountain' according to verse 45] without hands, which struck the image on its feet that were of iron and clay, and broke them in pieces. [35]Then the iron, the clay, the bronze, the silver, and the gold were broken in pieces together, and became like the chaff of the summer threshing floors. The wind carried them away, so that no place was found for them. The stone that struck the image became a great mountain, and filled the whole earth.

[36]"This is the dream; and we will tell its interpretation before the king. [37]You, O king, are king of kings, to whom the God of heaven has given the kingdom, the power, the strength, and the glory. [38]Wherever the children of men dwell, he has given the animals of the field and the birds of the sky into your hand, and has made you rule over them all. You are the head of gold.

³⁹"After you, another kingdom will arise that is inferior to you [In addressing the king of Babylon, Daniel couldn't avoid calling the nation who would conquer Babylon inferior]; and another third kingdom of bronze, which will rule over all the earth [This simply has to be Greece because Persia had famously failed to rule that part of the world]. ⁴⁰The fourth kingdom will be strong as iron, because iron breaks in pieces and subdues all things; and as iron that crushes all these, it will break in pieces and crush. [By the time critical scholars believe the book of Daniel was completed, Rome had already been crushing the Seleucid empire under a heavy war indemnity for over two decades, and she had very recently crushed a rebellion in Macedon, and broken up that home state of Alexander into four independent republics.] ⁴¹Whereas you saw the feet and toes, part of potters' clay, and part of iron, it will be a divided kingdom; but there will be in it of the strength of the iron, because you saw the iron mixed with miry clay. ⁴²As the toes of the feet were part of iron, and part of clay, so the kingdom will be partly strong, and partly broken. ⁴³Whereas you saw the iron mixed with miry clay, they will mingle themselves with the seed of men; but they won't cling to one another, even as iron does not mix with clay [Note that the division here is not into four parts, and therefore doesn't represent the Greek kingdoms – In fact, it is the bronze belly and two bronze thighs of the third empire (the world-ruling one) that most plausibly represents the Greek kingdoms of Macedon, Syria and Egypt (the relatively small kingdom of Pergamum being presumably represented by some other small body-part in that bronze region of the statue)].

⁴⁴"In the days of those kings the God of heaven will set up a kingdom which will never be destroyed, nor will its sovereignty be left to another people; but it will break in pieces and consume all these kingdoms, and it will stand forever. ⁴⁵Because you saw that a stone was cut out of the mountain without hands, and that it broke in pieces the iron, the bronze, the clay, the silver, and the gold; the great God has made known to the king what will happen hereafter. The dream is certain, and its interpretation sure."

The Four Monsters Dream (Daniel 7:1-28)

¹In the first year of Belshazzar king of Babylon Daniel had a dream and visions of his head on his bed. Then he wrote the dream and told the sum of the matters.

²Daniel spoke and said, "I saw in my vision by night, and, behold, the four winds of the sky broke out on the great sea. ³Four great animals came up from the sea, different from one another.

⁴"The first was like a lion, and had eagle's wings. I watched until its wings were plucked, and it was lifted up from the earth, and made to stand on two feet as a man. A man's heart was given to it.

⁵"Behold, there was another animal, a second, like a bear. It was raised up on one side, and three ribs were in its mouth between its teeth. They said this to it: 'Arise! Devour much flesh!'

⁶"After this I saw, and behold, another, like a leopard, which had on its back four wings of a bird. The animal also had four heads; and dominion was given to it.

⁷"After this I saw in the night visions, and, behold, there was a fourth animal, awesome and powerful, and exceedingly strong. It had great iron teeth. It devoured and broke in pieces, and stamped

the residue with its feet. It was different from all the animals that were before it. It had ten horns.

⁸"I considered the horns, and behold, there came up among them another horn, a little one, before which three of the first horns were plucked up by the roots: and behold, in this horn were eyes like the eyes of a man, and a mouth speaking great things.

⁹"I watched until thrones were placed, and one who was ancient of days sat. His clothing was white as snow, and the hair of his head like pure wool. His throne was fiery flames, and its wheels burning fire. ¹⁰A fiery stream issued and came out from before him. Thousands of thousands ministered to him. Ten thousand times ten thousand stood before him. The judgment was set. The books were opened.

¹¹"I watched at that time because of the voice of the great words which the horn spoke. I watched even until the animal was slain, and its body destroyed, and it was given to be burned with fire. ¹²As for the rest of the animals, their dominion was taken away; yet their lives were prolonged for a season and a time.

¹³"I saw in the night visions, and behold, there came with the clouds of the sky one like a son of man, and he came even to the ancient of days, and they brought him near before him. ¹⁴Dominion was given him, and glory, and a kingdom, that all the peoples, nations, and languages should serve him. His dominion is an everlasting dominion, which will not pass away, and his kingdom that which will not be destroyed.

¹⁵"As for me, Daniel, my spirit was grieved within my body, and the visions of my head troubled me. ¹⁶I came near to one of those who stood by, and asked him the truth concerning all this.

"So he told me, and made me know the interpretation of the things. ¹⁷'These great animals, which are four, are four kings [actually 'kingdoms' – see verse 23 – but perhaps 'kings' has been deliberately chosen to highlight the fact that each animal actually represents the spiritual ruler of the empire it represents], who will arise out of the earth. ¹⁸But the saints ['holy people' or 'devout followers'] of the Most High will receive the kingdom, and possess the kingdom forever, even forever and ever.'

¹⁹"Then I desired to know the truth concerning the fourth animal, which was different from all of them, exceedingly terrible, whose teeth were of iron, and its nails of bronze; which devoured, broke in pieces, and stamped the residue with its feet; ²⁰and concerning the ten horns that were on its head, and the other horn which came up, and before which three fell, even that horn that had eyes, and a mouth that spoke great things, whose look was more stout than its fellows [Other translations say 'more imposing']. ²¹I saw, and the same horn made war with the saints, and prevailed against them, ²²until the ancient of days came, and judgment was given to the saints of the Most High, and the time came that the saints possessed the kingdom.

²³"Thus he said, 'The fourth animal will be a fourth kingdom on earth, which will be different from all the kingdoms [which, of course, means it cannot be one of the four Greek kingdoms that are almost certainly represented by the leopard's four heads and wings], and will devour the whole earth, and will tread it down, and break it in pieces. [At the time critical scholars believe the book of Daniel was put together, Rome had already broken up the Greek kingdom of Macedon into four independent republics] ²⁴As for the ten horns, ten kings will arise out of this kingdom. Another will arise after them; and he will be different from the former, and he will put down three kings. ²⁵He will speak words against the Most High, and will wear out the saints of the Most High. He will plan to change the times and the law; and they will be given into his hand until a time and times and half a time.

²⁶" 'But the judgment will be set, and they will take away his dominion, to consume and to destroy it to the end. ²⁷The kingdom

and the dominion, and the greatness of the kingdoms under the whole sky, will be given to the people of the saints of the Most High [Notice here that it is not specifically the holy people themselves who receive this power but a people who would be *for* them – or at least, a people who would identify themselves as believers in their religion]. His kingdom is an everlasting kingdom, and all dominions will serve and obey him.'

[28]"Here is the end of the matter. As for me, Daniel, my thoughts much troubled me, and my face was changed in me; but I kept the matter in my heart."

The Seventy 'Sevens' Prophecy (Daniel 9:24-27)

[24]"Seventy weeks [or 'sevens' – almost all scholars accept that these are the weeks of seven years required by Leviticus 25:3-4] are decreed on your people and on your holy city, to finish disobedience, and to make an end of sins, and to make reconciliation for iniquity, and to bring in everlasting righteousness, and to seal up vision and prophecy, and to anoint the most holy [Note that this almost certainly means the 'most holy' is the 'Anointed One' in the next paragraph. Any other view ignores the fact that the content of the next paragraph is specifically stated to be an elucidation of the content of this one (that is why there are seventy 'sevens' mentioned in the next paragraph, and it is almost certainly also the reason that paragraph refers to an 'anointed one')].

[25]"Know therefore and discern that from the going out of the commandment [or 'word'] to restore and to build Jerusalem to the Anointed One ['Christ' in Greek], the prince [the Hebrew word is used for exalted popular leaders, including kings], will be seven weeks and sixty-two weeks [sixty-nine 'sevens']. It will be built again, with street and moat [in other words, both internally and with surrounding defenses], even in troubled times. [26]After the sixty-two weeks the Anointed One will be cut off [usually meaning 'put to death'], and will have nothing. The people of the prince who will come [another exalted leader or king] will destroy the city and the sanctuary. Its end [this can and is better translated 'His end' since a

pronoun is used in the next verse to refer to 'the prince who will come' as though the writer were continuing a discussion of that prince which had been ongoing throughout the previous verse] will be with a flood, and war will be even to the end. Desolations are determined. ²⁷He will make a firm covenant [most translations say 'confirm a covenant'] with many for one week. In the middle of the week he will cause the sacrifice and the offering to cease. On the wing [overspreading] of abominations will come one who makes desolate; and even to the full end, and that determined [or 'that is determined'], wrath will be poured out on the desolate [or desolator]." [Note that this translation of the last sentence does not make much sense (it suggests *two* endings that are 'determined', whereas only the end of the seventieth 'seven' is determined in the prophecy). Other translations render this final sentence as 'On an overspreading he will set up the abomination of desolation, even until the full end, that which is determined, is poured out him'. In other words, his death is the end that is determined. I think this is far more likely given the use of the term 'abomination of desolation' by the writer of Daniel 11:31 to refer to the idol set up by Antiochus Epiphanes (and by the writer of Matthew 24:15 in reference to this passage), and this rendering is strongly supported by the fact that the confirming of this prince's covenant is to end at 'the end determined' – the end of the seventieth 'seven'. This translation explains why, since it hints that this end is that prince's death].

The Ram and Goat Vision (Daniel 8:1-26)

¹In the third year of the reign of king Belshazzar a vision appeared to me, even to me, Daniel, after that which appeared to me at the first. ²I saw the vision. Now it was so, that when I saw, I was in the citadel of Susa, which is in the province of Elam. I saw in the vision, and I was by the river Ulai. ³Then I lifted up my eyes, and saw, and behold, there stood before the river a ram which had two horns. The two horns were high; but one was higher than the other, and the higher came up last. ⁴I saw the ram pushing westward, northward, and southward. No animals could stand before him. There wasn't any who could deliver out of his hand; but he did according to his will, and magnified himself.

⁵As I was considering, behold, a male goat came from the west over the surface of the whole earth, and didn't touch the ground. The goat had a notable horn between his eyes. ⁶He came to the ram that had the two horns, which I saw standing before the river, and ran on him in the fury of his power. ⁷I saw him come close to the ram, and he was moved with anger against him, and struck the ram, and broke his two horns. There was no power in the ram to stand before him; but he cast him down to the ground, and trampled on him. There was no one who could deliver the ram out

of his hand. ⁸The male goat magnified himself exceedingly. When he was strong, the great horn was broken; and instead of it there came up four notable horns toward the four winds of the sky [or 'of heaven'].

⁹Out of one of them came out a little horn [Antiochus IV Epiphanes], which grew exceeding great, toward the south, and toward the east, and toward the glorious land. ¹⁰It grew great, even to the army of the sky; and it cast down some of the army and of the stars to the ground, and trampled on them. ¹¹Yes, it magnified itself, even to the prince of the army [God]; and it took away from him the continual burnt offering, and the place of his sanctuary was cast down [This is exactly the same description of Epiphanes' actions as in Daniel 11:31]. ¹²The army was given over to it together with the continual burnt offering through disobedience. It cast down truth to the ground, and it did its pleasure and prospered.

¹³Then I heard a holy one speaking; and another holy one said to that certain one who spoke, "How long will the vision about the continual burnt offering, and the disobedience that makes desolate, to give both the sanctuary and the army to be trodden under foot be?"

¹⁴He said to me, "To two thousand and three hundred evenings and mornings. Then the sanctuary will be cleansed." [A temple cleansing did take place in 164 BC, after Judah Maccabee captured Jerusalem.]

¹⁵When I, even I Daniel, had seen the vision, I sought to understand it. Then behold, there stood before me something like the appearance of a man. ¹⁶I heard a man's voice between the banks of the Ulai, which called, and said, "Gabriel, make this man understand the vision."

¹⁷So he came near where I stood; and when he came, I was frightened, and fell on my face; but he said to me, "Understand, son of man; for the vision belongs to the time of the end."

¹⁸Now as he was speaking with me, I fell into a deep sleep with my face toward the ground; but he touched me, and set me upright.

¹⁹He said, "Behold, I will make you know what will be in the latter time of the indignation; for it belongs to the appointed time of the end. ²⁰The ram which you saw, that had the two horns, they are the kings of Media and Persia [Notice that the Medes and Persians are here represented by a single beast with a feature analogous to the higher and lower sides of the bear in Daniel 7]. ²¹The rough male goat is the king of Greece. The great horn that is between his eyes is the first king [Alexander the Great]. ²²As for that which was broken, in the place where four stood up, four kingdoms will stand up out of the nation, but not with his power [Might these not also be what the four heads and four bird-like wings on the leopard in Daniel 7 represent? – The bird-likeness of those wings, for example, could imply the comparative weakness mentioned here. In any case, the fact that four-part symbolism for Alexander's empire is clearly evident in this dream means it is extremely unlikely that the compiler of the book of Daniel would have regarded the four-headed, four-winged leopard in Daniel 7 as anything other than Alexander's empire. And since Rome was already the dominant nation in his day, and had decisively subdued all four Greek kingdoms, he was bound to consider the fourth monster in Daniel 7 to be Rome. As a result, there was no way he would regard the king represented by the eleventh horn on that monster as the Seleucid (Greek) king Antiochus Epiphanes. If that had been intended, he would have put those horns on one of the four heads of his leopard, just as the horn for Epiphanes in this vision grows out of one of the four horns of the goat].

²³"In the latter time of their kingdom, when the transgressors have come to the full, a king of fierce face, and understanding dark sentences, will stand up [Antiochus IV Epiphanes – Notice that there is no hint of eleven kings here, or three uprooted ones, which one would surely expect if the eleventh horn in Daniel 7 were thought by this writer to be Epiphanes as the critical consensus requires]. ²⁴His power will be mighty, but not by his own power [He was supported by the king of the Greek kingdom of Pergamum]. He will destroy

awesomely, and will prosper in what he does. He will destroy the mighty ones and the holy people. ²⁵Through his policy he will cause deceit to prosper in his hand. He will magnify himself in his heart, and he will destroy many in their security. He will also stand up against the prince of princes; but he will be broken without hand.

²⁶"The vision of the evenings and mornings which has been told is true; but seal up the vision, for it belongs to many days to come." [Here, as in Daniel 12:4, the prophet is told to 'seal up the vision' – thereby providing a means of explaining why nobody had heard of it before – a command that is notably absent from Daniel 2, 7 and 9].

From Alexander to Antiochus IV (Daniel 11:2-28)

²"Now I will show you the truth. Behold, three more kings will stand up in Persia; and the fourth will be far richer than all of them [Xerxes I]. When he has grown strong through his riches, he will stir up all against the realm of Greece [This almost certainly refers to Xerxes famous invasion of Greece in 480 BC which ended in his defeat at the battles of Salamis and Plataea. The prophecy then jumps forward 150 years to the rise of Alexander]. ³A mighty king will stand up [Alexander the Great], who will rule with great dominion, and do according to his will. ⁴When he stands up, his kingdom will be broken, and will be divided toward the four winds of the sky, but not to his posterity, nor according to his dominion with which he ruled; for his kingdom will be plucked up, even for others besides these [Again we have four weaker Greek kingdoms emerging from Alexander's empire].

⁵"The king of the south [Ptolemy I] will be strong. One of his princes [Seleucus I] will become stronger than him, and have dominion. His dominion will be a great dominion [the Seleucid Empire]. ⁶At the end of years [the end of the Second Syrian War] they will join themselves together; and the daughter [Berenice] of the king of the south [Ptolemy II] will come to the king of the north [Antiochus II] to make an agreement; but she will not retain the strength of her arm.

He will also not stand, nor will his arm; but she will be given up, with those who brought her, and he who became the father of her, and he who strengthened her in those times [Antiochus II, Berenice, and her infant son Antiochus all died at the hands of the exiled queen Laodice and her supporters in order for her to put her son Seleucus II on the throne. Ptolemy II dies around the same time.].

⁷"But out of a shoot from her roots one will stand up in his place [Berenice's brother Ptolemy III], who will come to the army, and will enter into the fortress of the king of the north [Seleucus II], and will deal against them, and will prevail. [Ptolemy III launched a very successful punitive campaign against Seleucus II known as the Third Syrian War]. ⁸He will also carry their gods, with their molten images, and with their goodly vessels of silver and of gold, captive into Egypt. He will refrain some years from the king of the north. ⁹He [Seleucus II] will come into the realm of the king of the south, but he will return into his own land [Seleucus II had to abandon his response to secure his remaining territory after a serious revolt split the Seleucid Empire]. ¹⁰His sons [Seleucus III and Antiochus III] will wage war, and will assemble a multitude of great forces, which will come on, and overflow, and pass through. They will return and wage war, even to his fortress.

¹¹"The king of the south [Ptolemy IV] will be moved with anger, and will come out and fight with him, even with the king of the north [now Antiochus III]. He [Antiochus III] will send out a great multitude, and the multitude will be given into his [Ptolemy IV's] hand [Battle of Raphia, 217 BC – the end of the Fourth Syrian War]. ¹²The multitude will be lifted up, and his heart will be exalted. He will cast down tens of thousands, but he won't prevail. ¹³The king of the north [Antiochus III again] will return, and will send out a multitude greater than the former. He will come on at the end of the times [around 200 BC! – the Fifth Syrian War], even of years, with a great army and with much substance.

¹⁴"In those times many will stand up against the king of the south [now Ptolemy V]. Also the children of the violent among your people will lift themselves up to establish the vision [What vision? Could the writer be referring to this vision to suggest that it existed thirty-five years before? Or could this refer to a premature attempt to fulfil Daniel 7 or 2?]; but they will fall. ¹⁵So the king of the north [Antiochus III still] will come and cast up a mound, and take a well-fortified city. The forces of the south [Ptolemy V] won't stand [Battle of Panium, 200 BC], neither will his chosen people, neither will there be any strength to stand. ¹⁶But he who comes against him [Antiochus III] will do according to his own will, and no one will stand before him. He will stand in the glorious land [Judea/Israel passed from Ptolemaic control to Seleucid control after the battle of Panium in 200 BC], and destruction will be in his hand. ¹⁷He [Antiochus III] will set his face to come with the strength of his whole kingdom, and with him equitable conditions. He [Ptolemy V] will perform them. He [Antiochus III] will give him the daughter of women [his daughter Cleopatra I], to corrupt her [make her act deceitfully for his gain]; but she will not stand, and won't be for him. ¹⁸After this he will turn his face to the islands, and will take many; but a prince [Roman general] will cause the reproach offered by him to cease. Yes, moreover, he will cause his reproach to turn on him [This refers to Rome's crushing victory over Antiochus III at the Battle of Magnesia in 189 BC, and the humiliating treaty of Apamea that followed. The latter secured Rome a constant flow of tribute, and the Seleucid heir as a hostage – even Antiochus IV Epiphanes spent time as a hostage of the Roman Senate before he took the Seleucid throne (and he wouldn't have been able to ascend that throne were it not for the fact that the rightful heir Demetrius remained in Rome)]. ¹⁹Then he will turn his face toward the fortresses of his own land; but he will stumble and fall, and won't be found.

²⁰"Then one [Seleucus IV] who will cause a tax collector [his general Heliodorus, who famously attempted to plunder the Jerusalem Temple to obtain the funds owed to Rome] to pass through the kingdom to maintain its glory will

stand up in his place; but within few days he shall be destroyed, not in anger, and not in battle [He was apparently assassinated by Heliodorus in an attempted coup].

21"In his place a contemptible person will stand up [Antiochus IV Epiphanes], to whom they had not given the honor of the kingdom; but he will come in time of security, and will obtain the kingdom by flatteries. 22The overwhelming forces will be overwhelmed from before him, and will be broken. Yes, also the prince of the covenant. 23After the treaty made with him he will work deceitfully; for he will come up, and will become strong, with a small people [probably the people of Pergamum]. 24In time of security he will come even on the fattest places of the province. He will do that which his fathers have not done, nor his fathers' fathers. He will scatter among them prey, plunder, and substance. Yes, he will devise his plans against the strongholds, even for a time.

25"He will stir up his power and his courage against the king of the south with a great army [Antiochus IV's first invasion of Egypt, 170 BC – the Sixth Syrian War]; and the king of the south [Ptolemy VI (or at least his guardians as he was just a child)] will wage war in battle with an exceedingly great and mighty army; but he won't stand; for they will devise plans against him. 26Yes, those who eat of his dainties will destroy him, and his army will be swept away. Many will fall down slain. 27As for both these kings, their hearts will be to do mischief, and they will speak lies at one table [After defeating and capturing Ptolemy VI, Antiochus attempted to make him his puppet king, rather than rule Egypt directly and risk alarming Rome, but within a year Ptolemy had rebelled]; but it won't prosper, for the end will still be at the appointed time. 28Then he will return into his land with great wealth. His heart will be against the holy covenant. He will take action, and return to his own land [This probably refers to Antiochus IV's plundering of the Jerusalem temple. His real persecution was after his second invasion of Egypt a year later – see p.119].

Antiochus IV Epiphanes (Daniel 11:29-12:12)

^{29}"He [Antiochus IV Epiphanes] will return at the appointed time, and come into the south [Egypt]; but it won't be in the latter time as it was in the former. ^{30}For ships of Kittim [Roman navy carrying the Senate's ambassador Gaius Popillius Laenas] will come against him. Therefore he will be grieved, and will return, and have indignation against the holy covenant [the Jewish faith], and will take action. He will even return, and have regard to those who forsake the holy covenant.

^{31}"Forces will stand on his part, and they will profane the sanctuary, even the fortress, and will take away the continual burnt offering [Epiphanes enforced Greek sacrifice in place of Jewish sacrifice at the Jerusalem Temple – He did not 'cause sacrifice to cease' there, but merely appropriated it for his god]. Then they will set up the abomination that makes desolate [An idol or altar to Zeus was set up in the Temple – A phrase almost certainly taken from Daniel 9 appears to have been used to describe this event]. ^{32}He will corrupt those who do wickedly against the covenant by flatteries; but the people who know their God will be strong, and take action.

^{33}"Those who are wise among the people will instruct many; yet they will fall by the sword and by flame, by captivity and by plunder, many days. ^{34}Now when they fall, they will be helped with a little help; but many will join themselves to them with flatteries. ³⁵Some of those who are wise will fall, to refine them, and to purify, and to make them white, even to the time of the end; because it is yet for the time appointed.

³⁶"The king will do according to his will. He will exalt himself, and magnify himself above every god, and will speak marvelous things against the God of gods. He will prosper until the indignation is accomplished; for that which is determined will be done. ³⁷He won't regard the gods of his fathers, or the desire of women, or regard any god; for he will magnify himself above all. ³⁸But in his place he will honor the god of fortresses. He will honor a god whom his fathers didn't know with gold, silver, and with precious stones and pleasant things. ³⁹He will deal with the strongest fortresses by the help of a foreign god. He will increase with glory whoever acknowledges him. He will cause them to rule over many, and will divide the land for a price.

⁴⁰"At the time of the end [Mainstream scholars suspect that the rest of this passage is the writer making a guess about the immediate future since Epiphanes did not invade Egypt a third time – It had to be quite detailed to convince the skeptics! I find it quite surprising that they don't ever suggest the same might apply to Daniel 2, 7 and 9.] the king of the south will contend with him; and the king of the north will come against him like a whirlwind, with chariots, with horsemen, and with many ships. He will enter into the countries, and will overflow and pass through [Note the flood metaphor of Daniel 9:27 being used to mean full-scale war]. ⁴¹He will enter also into the glorious land, and many countries will be overthrown; but these will be delivered out of his hand: Edom, Moab, and the chief of the children of Ammon. ⁴²He will also stretch out his hand on the countries. The land of Egypt won't escape. ⁴³But he will have power over the treasures of gold and of silver, and over all the precious things of Egypt. The Libyans and the Ethiopians will be at his steps. ⁴⁴But news out of the east and out of the north will

trouble him; and he will go out with great fury to destroy and utterly to sweep away many. ⁴⁵He will plant the tents of his palace between the sea and the glorious holy mountain; yet he will come to his end, and no one will help him.

¹²:¹"At that time Michael will stand up, the great prince who stands for the children of your people; and there will be a time of trouble, such as never was since there was a nation even to that same time. At that time your people will be delivered, everyone who is found written in the book. ²Many of those who sleep in the dust of the earth will awake, some to everlasting life, and some to shame and everlasting contempt. ³Those who are wise will shine as the brightness of the expanse. Those who turn many to righteousness will shine as the stars forever and ever. ⁴But you, Daniel, shut up the words, and seal the book, even to the time of the end. [Note here how the writer provides a reason for why nobody had heard of this prophecy before. A similar command occurs in Daniel 8:26. But intriguingly, there is no such command in Daniel 2, 7 or 9]. Many will run back and forth, and knowledge will be increased."

⁵Then I, Daniel, looked, and behold, two others stood, one on the river bank on this side, and the other on the river bank on that side. ⁶One said to the man clothed in linen, who was above the waters of the river, "How long will it be to the end of these wonders?"

⁷I heard the man clothed in linen, who was above the waters of the river, when he held up his right hand and his left hand to heaven, and swore by him who lives forever that it will be for a time, times, and a half; and when they have finished breaking in pieces the power of the holy people, all these things will be finished.

⁸I heard, but I didn't understand. Then I said, "My lord, what will be the outcome of these things?"

⁹He said, "Go your way, Daniel; for the words are shut up and sealed until the time of the end. ¹⁰Many will purify themselves, and make themselves white, and be refined; but the wicked will do wickedly; and none of the wicked will understand; but those who are wise will understand.

¹¹"From the time that the continual burnt offering is taken away, and the abomination that makes desolate set up, there will be one thousand two hundred and ninety days. ¹²Blessed is he who waits, and comes to the one thousand three hundred and thirty-five days.

¹³"But go your way until the end; for you will rest, and will stand in your inheritance at the end of the days."

OTHER BOOKS BY C. S. MORRISON

THE BLIND MINDMAKER

EXPLAINING CONSCIOUSNESS WITHOUT MAGIC OR MISREPRESENTATION

(2016) United States: CreateSpace Independent Publishing Platform
ISBN: 978-1541283954

"There is something very refreshing about this book.
It is free of the tired jargon of philosophy of mind.
It sticks to a scientific agenda in a way that a lot of scientists
would do well to emulate."

Jonathan C. W. Edwards
(Journal of Consciousness Studies, 24, No.7-8, 2017, p.237)

SURPRISED BY THE POWER OF DANIEL

THE MIRACLES THAT BROUGHT A SKEPTIC TO FAITH

(2018) United States: CreateSpace Independent Publishing Platform
ISBN: 978-1727668049

UNEXPECTEDLY FORETOLD OCCURRENCES

SCIENTIFIC EVIDENCE THAT THERE IS A GOD WHO LOVES YOU (AND WHY SCHOLARS DON'T DISCUSS IT)

(2016) United States: CreateSpace Independent Publishing Platform
ISBN: 978-1537728049

AUTHOR'S NOTE TO CHRISTIAN READERS

The views on the book of Daniel that are celebrated in my work are not those most commonly aired in church sermons. Since they have tremendously reinforced my faith in Christ, and are supported by all the textual, historical and archaeological evidence (making them very easy to defend against the claims of secular scholars), I believe this is a missed opportunity. I think Christian faith would be greatly strengthened wherever they did get preached. However, pastors generally avoid views on scripture that could be taken by some as casting doubt on its divine authorship. They will worry that many in their congregation might take offence at the claim that two of the prophecies scripture attributes to Daniel were actually written by a later impersonator. To some, this will seem irreconcilable with the notion that scripture is inspired by God ('God-breathed' according to 2 Tim. 3:16). I myself don't think it is in the least bit irreconcilable with that notion. I believe God inspired the impersonator to create these two prophecies just as he inspired the genuine Daniel to write the other three, and he did so for a very important function that could only be fulfilled by the writings of a later impersonator. They were put there to provide skeptical readers with a clear date from which they can be certain the three *genuine* Danielic prophecies were complete and in wide circulation, and to act as a key that ensures a rational interpreter cannot miss the fact that these prophecies accurately predicted the rise of Christianity and other rare and historically-significant events.

But wouldn't this mean that those scriptures were a lie? I don't think so. They would be lies if they had been intended to *deceive* us. However, they are so easy to recognise as forgeries that I don't believe we were ever meant to think they were authentic. On the contrary, with very little historical knowledge we can easily identify both their likely date of writing and their writer's view of the history that had unfolded since the time of Daniel. And we can thereby ascertain the meaning of the symbolism and obscure time phrases that Daniel's genuine prophecies incorporate. With a little more historical research one can then discover the truly astonishing accuracy of these genuine predictions.

Such objective proof of Christ's divinity is bound to bring many secular listeners to salvation. Nevertheless, pastors all-too-often don't want to change the status quo and risk already-committed believers leaving their church. Hence, in churches, the book of Daniel tends to be accepted without question as being all written by that named prophet (or contemporaries of his like king Nebuchadnezzar in Daniel 4). There are, of course, some scholars who support this assertion. However, they tend to belong to religious institutions that won't allow them to question it. If pastors were to ignore those scholars, they would gain an evangelistic tool far more effective than the loyalty of the few who leave as a result, and their confidence in the Gospel would be immensely magnified.

www.ingramcontent.com/pod-product-compliance
Lightning Source LLC
Chambersburg PA
CBHW070607050426
42450CB00011B/3012